THE WAY OF THE COURAGEOUS VULNERABLE

Finding Your Meaning & Purpose Through the 7 Stages of the Hero's Journey

Matthew Harris

Matthew Harris is an author, teacher and spiritual guide devoted to helping people access their innate wisdom, purpose and power.

He provides workshops, counselling, courses and retreats that help you experience your inherent wisdom, purpose and power.

To purchase books or inquire about programs, go to: courageousjourney.com.au

The Way of the Courageous Vulnerable: *Finding Your Meaning and Purpose Through the 7 Stages of the Hero's Journey* © Matthew Harris 2020

The moral rights of Matthew Harris to be identified as the author of this work have been asserted in accordance with the Copyright Act 1968

First published in Australia 2020 by _____

ISBN: 978-0-6488067-4-5

Any opinions expressed in this work are exclusively those of the author and are not necessarily the views held or endorsed by Matthew Harris.

All rights reserved. No part of this publication may be reproduced or transmitted by any means, electronic, photocopying or otherwise, without prior written permission of the author.

Disclaimer

All the information, techniques, skills and concepts contained within this publication are of the nature of general comment only and are not in any way recommended as individual advice. The intent is to offer a variety of information to provide a wider range of choices now and in the future, recognising that we all have widely diverse circumstances and viewpoints. Should any reader choose to make use of the information herein, this is their decision, and the author and publisher/s do not assume any responsibilities whatsoever under any conditions or circumstances. The author does not take responsibility for the business, financial, personal or other success, results or fulfilment upon the readers' decision to use this information. It is recommended that the reader obtain their own independent advice.

Table of Contents

Preface ix
Part 1: Overview 1
    Introduction 4
    The Hero's Journey – Overview. 7
    The Stages of the Journey. 9
    The Hero's Journey in Detail 10
Part 2: The Stages of the Journey 20
    Phase 1: Preparation and Departure 21
        Stage 1: Call to Adventure 30
        Stage 2: Crossing the Threshold 58
    Phase 2: Initiation 78
        Stage 3: The Road of Trials 79
        Stage 4: The Abyss. 126
        Stage 5: Rebirth and Transformation. 175
    Phase 3: The Return 196
        Stage 6: The Road Back, Rewards and Gifts 197
        Stage 7: Reintegration. 219
Conclusion 266
Acknowledgements 269
About the Author 270

Dedicated to all my teachers,
who have all contributed to my journey.
Thank you.

And to Sean Duncan Elias Harris – a beautiful boy with
a profound purpose. May you be blessed.

And still...

I walk my path...

Through places

I did not want to go.

Letting go

Of that which I did not want to release.

Becoming

That which I never thought I would be,

Greater

Than I ever knew,

Freer

Than I ever hoped.

Always

I Am.

And still...

I walk my path...

Artist: Leo Plaw, Arise

Hero: A person who is admired for their courage, outstanding achievements, or noble qualities. They personify a nobility of spirit which manifests as concern and compassion for others and the well-being of all.

Courage: The quality of mind or spirit (mental or moral strength) that enables a person to venture, persevere, or face difficulty, danger, pain, or fear.

"Courage is a heart word. The root of the word courage is *cor* - the Latin word for heart. In one of its earliest forms, the word courage meant "To speak one's mind by telling all one's heart."

Brene Brown, Author

Vulnerable: Open or exposed to the possibility of being wounded or harmed.

Ordinary: What is commonplace or standard.

Preface

"Just see if you can enjoy being sick", my brother said to me as I lay on the couch sweating from a virus that I had had for a week. I cursed him under my breath as I acknowledged the absurd logic of what he said. He was right.

He was saying there was a flow in which I could choose to sit, that allowed the virus to naturally go through my body. If I could just allow and even enjoy this process, then I would do much better. The virus would do its thing in my body and then leave. However, if I spent my time fighting the virus by trying hard to make something happen, it would probably linger longer, prolonging my discomfort.

In 1999, I experienced an emotional breakdown. It was on a scale I had never experienced before. It was triggered by me seeing my ex-wife from across the street. There was nothing special at all about this event. She was having lunch with friends and appeared to be having a good time. We were divorced the year before, and it was always uncomfortable seeing her at that time. It always stirred up butterfly feelings in my stomach; feelings of not knowing what to do, say, or feel.

On this day, I saw her from across the street and again felt the same feelings of discomfort and uncertainty. This time, however, it was a little more intense than usual. This time, there was an accompanying feeling of nausea and a higher level of uncertainty, and I'm sure my breath was shorter and there was a tightness in my chest and stomach. I wasn't sure whether to go over and speak to her, to deal with the situation in front of me, or to acknowledge how I felt and go home. I decided just to go home and allow my body and my feelings to settle, even though I felt a bit defeated in not speaking with her.

But my feelings didn't settle. I experienced a level of nausea and emotional and energetic build-up I had never before encountered. I had had several emotional breakdowns in the past, the first being when I was 19, but this had an intensity and depth and breadth which was completely new to me. It was incredibly unsettling. I was confused about what was happening to me. It felt like I was stepping into something huge and I had no frame of reference for what was occurring.

And then it happened. The dam to my emotions broke open. It was an opening to grief, shame and sadness that I had never experienced before. I had been through many periods of depression and sadness before, but I had never felt such intensity in the upwelling of emotion, over which I had no control at all. I couldn't ignore it and I couldn't suppress it; it was just too big. I knew the best thing I could do was to feel these feelings, as uncomfortable as they were, and allow them to pass through my body.

The intensity of shame and sadness I felt drew me to my knees. I wept and wept and cried and sobbed from the hurt and shame I felt, down to the bottom of my guts. The sensations and overwhelm went on for more than an hour. They just kept on coming, longer than ever before. Eventually, the intensity eased, and I was able to get up and try to work out what was going on.

From my previous experience with depressive episodes, I knew there was an intelligence going on which I needed to attune myself to. I knew that these episodes resolve in their own time, and it means allowing for the movement of the accompanying energies. As time went on, these episodes of grief and sadness emerged spontaneously during the day or night. Eventually, I had to resign from my job as I could no longer perform my work functionally. I had to pay attention to my healing, and do it now.

In doing so, I sought out healers and therapists of different modalities. I began meditating, enrolled in personal development courses and allowed myself to feel deeply what was going on within me. It was a profoundly uncomfortable and painful period.

But it was also a time filled with deep insights and personal revelations. I was uncovering long-held suppressed feelings and emotions from deep within me. They lead me to a greater understanding of who I was, and what happened to me through my life. I was shown where my responsibility lay for the pain I was experiencing. This breakdown was creating a *breakthrough* for me into a deeper appreciation of myself and the world around me.

In 2000, during my healing process, I experienced several profound intuitive insights. One of them was to trust the 'still, small voice' that occasionally spoke to me. This voice was my intuition, an angelic presence, and I knew its voice was true. I knew its truth because it was clear, it was still, and it was certain. There was no pressure or judgement with it.

One evening, after a series of meditations over the previous week, this intuitive voice told me to change my name in order to embody the changes I had experienced in my healing. I was, both symbolically and manifestly, becoming a new person.

So, in October 2000 I changed my name. I crossed a threshold and walked into the world as a new person. At the time, I had great hopes and dreams of a new life with my new name, embodying freedom, wealth and love. I believed I would leave the painful past behind and walk a new path of personal power, freedom and abundance. Little did I know however, that life, had a completely different plan to the one I had in mind.

Just a few years later, life's plan for me led me to experience extended periods of illness (perpetual viruses including glandular fever), unemployment, poverty, isolation, failure and depression. I seemed unable to achieve anything, even though I was doing all the right things the personal development courses told me to: have goals, write them down, make them SMART, meditate, think positive, read books, be in a Mastermind group, find a mentor and take action. None of these things seemed to work. I felt totally powerless and ineffectual. In fact, some methods like positive thinking actually made me feel *worse*. I felt like either I was either always doing something wrong, or there must be something wrong with me.

Paradoxically, even though I was experiencing failure and depression, I always had a sense that there was something within me, assuring me that I was alright and that 'I' was not my circumstances, and that I was actually on a profound journey of purpose. I always felt that there was a *light* within me, some inexplicable energy or force, leading me on to achieve a purpose which I couldn't comprehend at the time.

I experienced immense feelings of frustration and hopelessness during this time. I was doing my best to create a vision and goals, and take action accordingly. But I always seemed to go nowhere along that path. I felt like I lived in a landscape where there was mud to the horizon in all directions, and whatever I did, however I plodded, nothing changed. And it went on for years. And years. And years.

Eventually, after years of struggle and my brother saying that I should "...just try and enjoy being sick", I slowly learnt the lesson and stopped trying to control the process. Eventually, I found ways to be at ease with my journey and appreciate myself and others around me. I finally realised that there was a bigger purpose and journey I was living through, or was living through me, I just didn't know what it was. And even though I wasn't achieving my goals and dreams, I was still part of a much grander purpose which I couldn't fathom at the time.

By 2013, I realised that I had completed this journey. I had fulfilled the purpose of that part of my life. It was the end of a huge and important cycle in my life. I had been through an arduous journey that had taken me into an abyss of depression, failure, powerlessness, illness, poverty and humiliation many times, over many years. I had completed a full Hero's Journey cycle.

During 2012 I knew this cycle was coming to an end, and by 2013, I knew I completed it. I knew that I had done all that I was supposed to do, and that I had been on a profound journey of healing and transformation. I had emerged as a new being into the light of a new day. I was so relieved. I had completed a major part of my life's purpose, and I felt free. I realised that the name I had adopted during that period was a persona I needed to embody, to enable me, Matthew, to emerge at the end. So again, the inner voice of *knowing* called to me and affirmed that I should change my name, back to my birth name. And so, I did.

I realised that I had completed a full cycle of the Hero's Journey. I had lived in the *Known World, Crossed Thresholds*, encountered *allies and enemies*, endured many *Trials and Challenges*, and had been into the *Abyss* and experienced death and rebirth, multiple times. I had then emerged into the path of *Ascent*.

On the *Ascent*, I gained new insights and appreciations of myself and others. I put these insights into action as sincerely as I could in my work and personal life. I gained new allies and enemies, and endured even greater trials and temptations, as I was challenged to endure further illness, poverty and powerlessness.

But finally, finally the challenges ended and I emerged from my journey into a new sense of health, freedom and empowerment. I emerged into a realisation that my life was an expression of a profound purpose of healing and transmutation which was unrecognised by myself and others as I was going through it.

The focus of my appreciation and insight was that most people, however ordinary, are far more courageous and noble than we give them credit for. And that we, as ordinary as we are, are far more courageous and noble than we give ourselves credit for. And we perform these courageous and noble acts in our very ordinary daily lives.

I understand now that we may not be able to control our circumstances, but we do have some choice in how we experience them. If we face our hardship and powerlessness with acceptance, courage and nobility, we can then emerge from our journey bringing greater peace, wisdom and love into the world. Or we can traverse it with avoidance, cynicism and bitterness.

In response to this momentous life event, I started writing short articles and posting them on social media. I wrote about my insights and my appreciation of people and the courage and nobility they exhibited in their ordinary lives. I spoke of how our ordinary experiences, from hardship to achievement, from the profound to the mundane, are part of a great journey that occurs naturally in our lives. I wanted to share my perception that even when we go through our lowest moments, or performing the most mundane of tasks, we can still be fulfilling our life's purpose.

A Book, a Calling and the Hero's Journey

I knew that a book was calling me, but I didn't know how to start or what to do. So, I just started writing. I wrote short pieces about my insights and awareness and posted them on social media. I wrote intuitively, often stimulated by my responses to others on social media.

What I brought was a depth and appreciation which I drew from my experience. These personalised reflections were quite different to the common articles posted about positive thinking or spiritual truths at the time. These articles have formed the basis of this book.

Having endured extended periods of depression, ill health, poverty and powerlessness over many years, I realised that there was both purpose and meaning behind my experiences. I found an explanation and illustration of that purpose through the Hero's Journey template.

I have used the Hero's Journey template as an organising tool for the articles. The template is useful because it is both personal and universal. It is both symbolic and practical, and easily applicable to our ordinary and material lives. It applies to all people, whatever their gender, to describe the commonality of the different stages of our life's journey.

This book then describes these natural and grand cycles that occur in our ordinary lives and the way they affect us through challenges and achievements. They show us that our journey achieves grand and noble ends, that both build and reveal our character, and delivers our legacy and our purpose through our ordinary lives.

So now, in gathering my writings and sharing my insights, I hope that you too will find greater self-awareness and self-appreciation as you go through your journey. And please, take it from me, as you go through your journey, *just see if you can enjoy being sick.*

PART ONE:

THE HERO'S JOURNEY OVERVIEW

> *"The Hero's Journey is not an invention, but an observation. [It is] nothing less than a handbook for life, a complete instruction manual in the art of being human."*
>
> **Christopher Vogler**
> **The Writer's Journey – Mythic Structure for Writers**

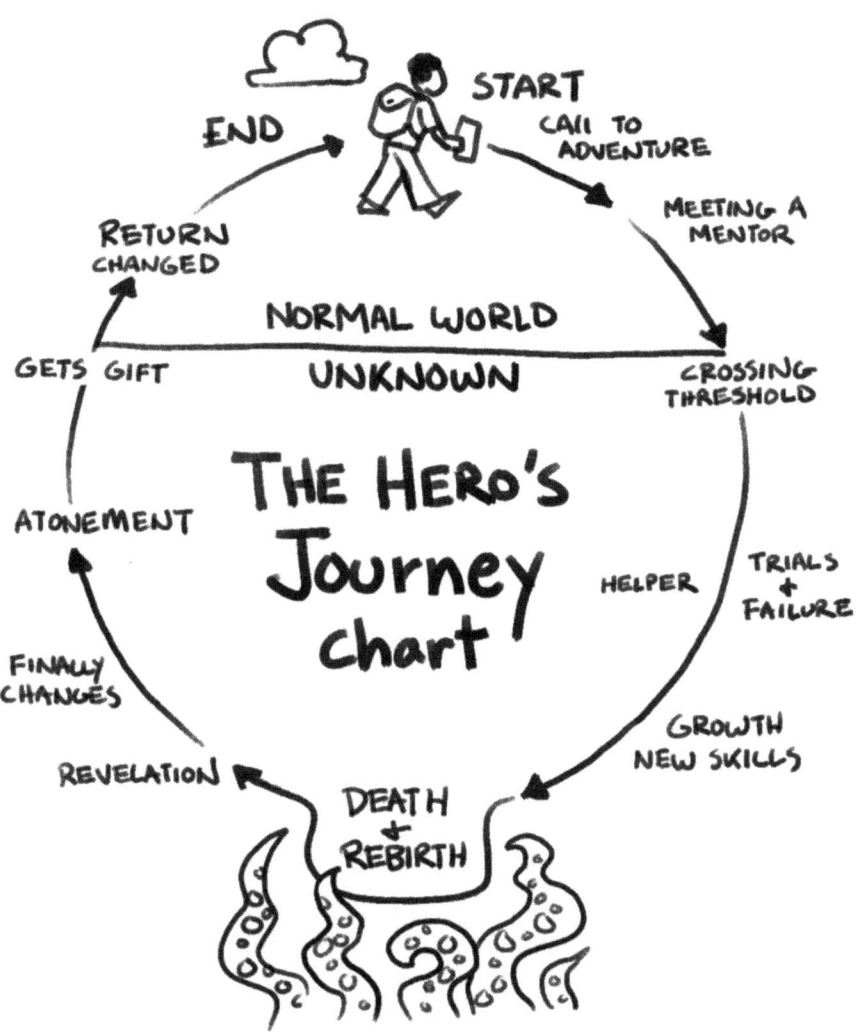

INTRODUCTION

The Hero's Journey - It's Universal

I love the Hero's Journey. I was formally introduced to it in 2010 when I attended a Transpersonal Counselling course. As it was being explained, I could see how my life's experiences could fit within it. I could see how my life fitted within a grand plan, and I immediately gained a sense of relief from that moment.

I love how it simply and actively provided a template and meaning for my life's journey. I could see how my experience of 'failure', illness and turmoil could fit easily within the Initiation stage of this template.

I could see how falling in love and getting married was me 'Crossing a Threshold', and there were Mentors and Guides in other areas assisting me on the way. I could see the Temptations and distractions that were taking me off track, and I could see the times I entered the Abyss and experienced death. And then, following that, those times of Rebirth, of new awareness and relief from past burdens.

I love also how it shows me how archetypes, symbols and mythology express themselves in my life, and how these basic and universal elements are still relevant to me today.

I realised then, that as a kid, my interest in ancient stories of myths and legends was actually initiating me into the world of the Hero's Journey, archetypes and symbols, without knowing it.

The Hero's Journey is clearly demonstrated through age-old stories in many different cultures, like the tales of King Arthur, the Arabian Nights, and the Mahabharata. And now it is being used in movies, video games and TV series, from the likes of The Lord of the Rings, Game of Thrones, Japanese anime, and even the Toy Story animation movies.

Joseph Campbell first described universal characteristics in stories and folktales that occurred across cultures and across time in his 1949 book, The Hero with a Thousand Faces. Later, these universal stages became known as the Hero's Journey. Later again, an American family therapist called Maureen Murdoch, found additional elements relating to the way of the feminine in our modern life journeys, and called it The Heroine's Journey, as outlined in her 1990 book.

Both involve the Hero (female or male) moving through different stages of their life's journey. They encounter trials and challenges, a descent into profound emotional, physical and spiritual turmoil, and eventually into atonement and reconciliation with themselves and the world. This brings new-found gifts, boons and wisdom back into the community and the world.

It is important to note that both the Hero and the Journey are **not** gender specific. They are universal, and thereby archetypal in their nature and experience. Both women and men are heroes of their own life's journey and may experience all the different elements of the Hero's Journey and the Heroine's Journey in their lifetime.

There are three well-known parts of the Journey. They are: Part 1 - Preparation in the Known World and Departure from it, Part 2 - going on the journey into Initiation that brings successes, trials and challenges, and that eventually leads through an Abyss into discovering your true gifts and talents. From here, the Hero begins Part 3 – the Return: a path of ascension where your new talents and gifts are tested, and then brought forth as wisdom, to Return into the world, and fulfil your soul's purpose.

Where Do You See the Hero's Journey?

It is easy to see this playing out in movies, books and TV shows. The whole journey is played out in a character's developmental arc in a compressed period of time. It's more difficult to see it in your own life though, as you are the character in your own movie.

But the Hero's Journey does play out in our own lives. We live in a Known World; a family, a business or a common pattern of thinking. We often receive Calls to Adventure as we get messages, interventions or invitations to do something new. We must make decisions about Crossing the Threshold to engage the new experience, or not. And we often experience Trials and Challenges (illnesses, uncertainties, and failures), and then decide how to engage with them in the new Unknown World.

So, what do you do in these testing circumstances? How do you respond? How do you decide what to do and which way to go? The Hero's Journey asks profound questions of you as you encounter these turning points.

The Journey asks you to engage with questions like: Who are you when you don't get what you want? Do you hoard your new talents and gifts? Are you afraid they are going to be taken away from you? Who do you trust? Can you trust yourself and others, when you have experienced profound betrayal and hardship in your life?

I find the Hero's Journey fascinating and enlivening. It has helped me see myself, and those around me, as people of great courage and heart, with talents and abilities that are both expressed and undiscovered, that are part of a great cycle and journey of fulfilment and achievement. These ordinary people, going through their ordinary lives, are also very heroic, noble and courageous.

How the Hero's Journey Affects You?

The Hero's Journey is a series of stages, set out in a natural cycle. It helps you see and experience the world symbolically and mythologically within a universal and timeless framework.

The Hero's Journey affects you whether you are a woman or a man, old or young, successful or going through hard times. It is a cycle that is present in your circumstances, in your decisions, in your feelings and in your thinking. It is a template, a guide to describe the different stages you are going through in your life. It is telling you that You are the Hero of your own life's journey.

The next chapters describe in more detail what the Hero's Journey is, and how it appears in your life.

The Hero's Journey - Overview

The Hero's Journey in Your Ordinary Life

Most people live very ordinary lives: they go to work, go shopping, take the kids to school, go home, watch TV, prepare meals and make decisions about where to spend their time and money. Most people make sacrifices for others, endure hardships, illness, unfairness, challenges and losses, as well as experiencing times of happiness, achievement, success and love.

All of these things are part of The Hero's Journey; your successes, your losses, your dreams, your decisions and thoughts are all part of a much bigger process and journey of life.

By taking the time to learn about the Hero's Journey and the archetypes that go with it, you can find a way to appreciate yourself and your life's journey more fully. You can see there are patterns and cycles at play, that seem to demonstrate a much bigger design and set of principles within your life.

Understanding the Hero's Journey allows you to see your life as fulfilling a far grander purpose than you can see at the time. It shows you that going through your periods of hardship and struggle, as well as and your successes and achievements, are all a natural and normal part of your journey. And the purpose of the journey is to provide the opportunity for you to develop your character and fulfil your soul's mission.

Who is This Book For?

This book is for people at all stages of their life's journey: it is a Call to Adventure for those just beginning a journey; it provides comfort for those enduring the hardships of the Initiation phase; and it provides meaning and context to those who have experienced the fullness of the journey and are now at The Return, looking for ways to pass on their experience and wisdom.

Engaging with the Hero's Journey means you are willing to go through the process that takes you through darkness and uncertainty, and employ the courage needed to deal with the challenges you will face. It will often call you to move into your heart, to uncover and heal painful wounds, and then emerge from this place of vulnerability into a new strength and capability. This is the path of the Courageous Vulnerable, and it is a Hero's Journey taking place in your ordinary life.

I have also included several humorous pieces in the book. This is to show that humour is a normal and natural part of your spiritual and personal development too. The way of the Fool archetype, which is strong with me, is one of the brightest, wisest and most courageous of the archetypes. The Fool enables you to break down internal barriers and resistance to your circumstances. Finding laughter and absurdity in your life can allow the old ways to leave and new ways of perception and being to come in. For example, how many times after crying deeply and miserably, have you then started laughing?

In reading this book, I hope you gain greater appreciation for yourself and the journey you have been on. I hope you appreciate the many courageous paths you have followed and choices you have made throughout your life. I hope you see and appreciate that even through those times of hardship and uncertainty, there was a path of destiny calling you to embody your highest self. And I hope you can then see all those elements in the people around you too. The ordinary people around you, who also live courageous and heroic lives.

This book can work for you, either by reading it from start to finish, or opening it randomly and gaining insights into different elements of your life from there. However you choose to read it, please enjoy and gain the insights, meaning and purpose you will uncover and discover in The Way of the Courageous Vulnerable.

The Stages of the Journey

Part One: Preparation and Departure.
All stories open in the Hero's Known World.
There are commonly two main events which occur:
1. The Call to Adventure, and the gaining of Mentors, Helpers and Guides.
2. Crossing the Threshold.

Part Two: Initiation.
Initiation sees the Hero cross a significant threshold and moves into the Unknown World. This stage has many powerful life-changing events within it:
3. The Road of Trials – challenges, temptations, allies and enemies.
4. The Abyss – the place of darkness, despair and symbolic or actual death.
5. Rebirth and Transformation.

Part Three: The Return.
The Hero returns to the Known World, but this time as a transformed being. They now bear the gifts and wisdom from their journey. These gifts, when applied within the community, bring healing, restoration and reconciliation.
6. The Road Back, Rewards and Gifts.
7. Reintegration.

The Hero's Journey in Detail

Part One: Preparation and Departure

Preparation starts in the Known World where everything appears to follow a familiar pattern. Characters behave as expected, as does our Hero (You). Think of the opening of The Lord of the Rings where we see Frodo going about his normal, ordinary business, meeting and greeting people and performing his duties.

Then a crisis, intervention or message occurs. This is the Call to Adventure. This may appear as unexpected relationship breakdowns, a job loss, health issues or injustices. Or it may be a message or invitation to go somewhere new or different. You may be invited to meet someone or receive a job offer or a new opportunity. In the movie Star Wars, Luke Skywalker received an unexpected message from R2D2 about a mysterious Princess asking for help. Or in the movie Harry Potter and The Philosopher's Stone, Harry receives letters delivered by magical owls.

The upshot is that the Hero (You), **must** depart their Known World. If you refuse, then somehow you will be compelled, expelled, or banished from your environment, thus ensuring you go on your journey, however unfair that may seem to be. During this stage, you may be accompanied by a Mentor or Guide, such as Obi Wan Kenobi in Star Wars, or Hagrid in Harry Potter, or Glinda the Good Witch for Dorothy in the Wizard of Oz.

The Hero (You) may sometimes resist this departure and spend time and energy trying to get back into their Known World to defeat the injustice and restore their name. However, it never works, and you must turn around, accept the reality of your situation, and walk into the unknown. This is where you literally Cross a Threshold into a new Unknown World.

In your own life, you may go through this stage many times. It is where you may live with a sense of comfort or ease, or like Harry Potter, the world is painful and unfair. At some point, something happens that will ask you to make an important decision: Do you stay, or do you go?

You go. You make a definite decision and you leave your Known World. You venture into the unknown. This decision may be to escape hardship and injustice or to engage opportunity, but either way, you leave.

Part Two: The Journey into Initiation

This is where the Hero (You) finds their way into a new world. At first, supported by their mentor and new allies, the Hero (You) progresses through the world engaging in new challenges, and acquiring new knowledge and skills. But soon, you meet with temptations, trials and enemies.

In The Lord of the Rings, Frodo, Merry, Pippin and Sam meet with the Black Riders as they leave the Shire. They know viscerally that they are not just on a simple jaunt across the fields anymore. In Harry Potter, Harry meets Malfoy and Professor Snape, giving him a strong sense that he is dealing with powerful forces aligned against him.

In your own life, you may have started a new job, and others in that environment have already staked their territory and control over pathways to approval, procedure and success. You may find that you do not have the resources or support to achieve your goals. Or in relationships, you see the signs that your partner might not be the idealised person you want or believe them to be, and that your expectations may not be met.

The purpose of the Preparation and Departure stage of the journey is to prepare you for the profound transformation that is to come. It is where the Hero (You) learns and finally experiences the limitations of who they are and what they believe in. The Journey eventually takes you on a path to find the essence of your true power and abilities. But this can only happen through your inevitable humbling. The Initiation is a path into your vulnerability, into your courage, into your depth, and then embracing all that arises, you emerge through it.

Your journey through Initiation takes you on a path where the pressures increase to test you in your old ways of thinking, perceiving and being. Relationships will be strained, jobs and work may cease and hardships, sickness and injustices may be keenly felt. All the old ways, beliefs and perceptions cease to work, or don't produce the results they used to. Pressure and stress inevitably increase as pathways and choices narrow, putting your internal coping mechanisms under intense strain.

All of this leads inexorably to an Abyss, the place of darkness and (symbolic) death. It is a hellish path, as old fears, anxieties, wounds and deeply held denials are brought up and exposed. These wounds reveal deeply held and repressed feelings and beliefs, like being unloved, not being good enough, abandoned or betrayed by family or trusted allies. This is the place of absolute despair. It is the place of death and metamorphosis. It is through the Ordeal which the Hero, that you release all your attachments to your old identity, dreams and goals. All of it all must go. **All** of it.

This is the essential meaning of the great hardships you go through. The pressure, the darkness, the isolation, the feeling that you are being torn apart, is all there to get you to this place of Abyss; the place of annihilation, transformation, metamorphosis, and then finally, emergence.

Eventually, there comes a transformation and a new life; a Rebirth. The simple essence of this stage, the Abyss and Ordeal, is that the Hero (You) **must** die to be reborn and transformed. This often occurs with the assistance of a mentor, a guide or a magical force.

You then begin your ascent and your journey to Return to the World. This is often just as arduous as the previous journey of descent, as now you must apply and embody the new skills, gifts and knowledge you developed as the new person you are becoming.

Again, there are great challenges as You (the Hero) ascends into your new life. You may move to a different suburb or city. You may leave your previous employment and obtain new work, or you may leave a long-standing relationship. Either way, old ways are discarded in favour of adopting new methods and ways of being, that don't just benefit you, the individual, but bring benefits to a wider community. You are beginning a life of service.

Eventually, there is also an Atonement. That is where the Hero (You) is humbled again and expresses sorrow, seeks forgiveness or redemption from someone they have harmed in some way in their life. This stage creates an opening for the redemption of others too, as the weight of past errors and transgressions is lifted. This is the heart of the Initiation. It is the confrontation with figures of ultimate power in your life. It is the subjugation of your ego-self, to a greater power or purpose in your life. It is testing your commitment to your new life of service.

There will also be Temptations to draw you away from your true path and back to the old ways. This could be in the form of a job offer to go back to the old firm, or an old relationship returns, or the offer of money and riches on a completely different path to distract you, the Hero.

But eventually, the Hero (You) deals with these temptations by demonstrating and embodying your new awareness and values by making decisions that are aligned with your new Self.

And finally, Part Three: The Return

Again, you Cross a Threshold to bring You (the Hero) back into the community. This can also be fraught with difficulty as you may struggle with leaving the world you now know well, to go back to your previous Known World. But you move through your resistance and commit to returning to your former home to apply the gifts and rewards you acquired on your journey. This is done humbly, with respect and appreciation, in service to, and in accordance with the revelations you have received. You do this even though you may not be appreciated. This becomes your stage of Reintegration, sovereignty, and freedom.

This is where Sam and Frodo, Merry and Pippin return to the Shire to take on positions of responsibility within the community. In Star Wars, it is where Princess Leia accepts her role as leader of the New Republic. It is where Harry Potter, Hermione and Ron, and even Draco Malfoy, walk back into the world of Hogwarts and the mundane, after their world-saving adventures. They do so by accepting the parameters of their ordinary lives in the world. They accept and appreciate that living in the ordinary and mundane, is a beautiful and powerful way to live.

This is the Hero's Journey. It is a path that initiates you on a journey to accept your true talents and calling. It is a Call to Adventure, that inevitably leads you on a path into your greatness, that is expressed through your ordinariness.

I know many people who have been, or are going through this cycle. They have been through the Journey or Initiation stage. This is often the hardest times of their lives, where they may have lost everything, and are now emerging from long periods of incubation and recalibration, into the Return. They bring a holistic awareness and appreciation of themselves and the world, and an understanding that they cannot have a new beginning without first going through the ending. This is the courage of the ordinary. This is the courage of living through your vulnerability, and bringing that wisdom and those gifts, into your life.

The Archetypes

Archetypes are personal, ancient, and universal symbols and images that depict patterns of thought, energy and power. They are essential in any discussion of the Hero's Journey. They are metaphorical images of people or circumstances of the literal things in our lives. They are easily illustrated in examples like the King, Queen, Mother, Child, Fool, Sage, or Warrior. They are also life events like Birth, Initiation, Death, or Rebirth.

Archetypes become powerful symbols of growth when you can see them playing out in your life. It's easy to identify them in movies and books, and it is these universal qualities that show you why TV shows like Game of Thrones, Breaking Bad and Merlin are so popular worldwide. Archetypes are ever present in movies like The Matrix, Bladerunner, Star Wars and the Wizard of Oz, and even children's animations like The Incredibles have worldwide appeal.

The Hero's Journey is always about a journey to discover and uncover the treasures within your true self and bring these gifts and talents into the world. The archetypes such as the Warrior, the Hero, the Child, and the Magician are all an integral part of this journey of discovery, initiation and integration.

THE HERO'S JOURNEY IN DETAIL

In Carol Pearson's wonderful book, Awakening the Heroes Within, she details the role that twelve major archetypes play in your journey. She has grouped these archetypes according to the stage of the journey they apply most. They are:

Preparation and Departure: Innocent, Orphan, Warrior, Caregiver

The Journey into Initiation: Seeker, Destroyer, Lover, Creator

The Return: Sovereign (Queen/King), Magician, Sage, Fool

Preparation and Departure:

The first four archetypes assist you in preparing for your Journey. You begin as an Innocent, a Child, naïve and optimistic, with innate hope and trust. As you encounter hardships, failures, and betrayals you become an Orphan. That is, in experiencing betrayal, lack of support and comfort, you learn that you are alone in the world. Here you strengthen your ego and learn about willpower, determination and perseverance.

Your Warrior then comes to the fore by setting boundaries or shields, and creating goals and developing strategies to achieve them. As you move through this stage, your Caregiver is activated as you learn to care for others and eventually yourself, or moves into Shadow as you adopt strategies to survive such as being a Rebel, putting up barriers, cladding yourself in armour and becoming cynical.

In movies, Luke Skywalker in Star Wars, Frodo in The Lord of the Rings and Dorothy in The Wizard of Oz, exemplify these archetypes. All three are literally orphans, and all exhibit qualities of the Innocent – idealistic and naïve, with a strong sense of justice. All receive a Call to Adventure and are thrust into a new path despite their protestations. Once they accept the Call, they are compelled to go on their journey. Their Warrior archetype is activated through their determination and acts of self-preservation, but it is tempered by having a strong Caregiver, as demonstrated by their loyalty to friends, family, and the community.

The Journey into Initiation:

Through your sense of *calling*, you become the Seeker of the things, skills and knowledge that will serve you on your journey. This means you may study subjects or attend workshops, read books, or find work in a field that is aligned with your *calling*. Hence, many people study yoga or health practices, begin careers or take up hobbies aligned with their calling. In movies, you see Luke Skywalker learning to wield a light-sabre, and begin experiencing the reality of the Force. Similarly, you learn new skills and paradigms of thought and perception in a new job or relationship, and then apply them in your daily life.

The Destroyer is a natural part of the journey as you encounter hardships and failures that take away things that were previously thought essential to your identity. This could be your job, relationships, house, income or status. Symbolically, through these circumstances you encounter death. This is the Road of Trials and is an Initiation through suffering. These trials both strengthen your ego, and paradoxically, enable it to break down, as it then serves a Higher Purpose.

This is where Dorothy's allies in the Wizard of Oz all experience catastrophes of some sort by literally having the stuffing taken out of them (Scarecrow), freezing up and losing all mobility (Tin Man), and experiencing intense cowardice, anxiety and fear (Lion). The Destroyer has come into their lives to show them that there are forces in the world beyond their control.

This stage is complemented by a pathway directed by the Lover archetype. It leads you to begin caring about people, causes or values that serve your calling or higher purpose. It activates a deeper sense of love and passion within you that requires commitment and engagement with others. It is exemplified by Samwise Gamgee in The Lord of the Rings by his devotion to Frodo and their quest. This activation of love and care within you ensures you experience a rebirth; the creation of a new self. This then activates the treasure you were seeking all along. But, it's not 'out there' where you thought it was, it is within you.

The Creator archetype then arises, and helps you express your new self in the world. It aligns your actions, thoughts and values with your underlying purpose. You are being led into alignment and in service to your *calling*.

We see this in The Matrix when Neo fights Smith for the first time, instead of running away, as everyone else has done. He is stepping into his role as 'The One' in this new world, a notion he had previously rejected. As Morpheus, Neo's mentor observes, "He is beginning to believe." All these qualities are needed as you experience The Return to the Known World.

The Return

As you take responsibility for yourself and your world, you activate the Sovereign or Queen/King archetype in your life. You do this by accepting that you are responsible for your life and how you live it. You may then take on more responsibility at work or within your relationships. You may ensure the maintenance and good working of your household and workplace; that is, your 'realm'. And, most importantly, you may finally attend to creating a healthy relationship with yourself. By doing so, you are moving into your maturity and demonstrating your sense of service to the community, and to your greater purpose, by paradoxically attending to your own needs first.

You activate the Magician in your life by attending to your healing, transformation, creativity, and your relationship with nature and spirit. Yoda and Obi Wan Kenobi from Star Wars personify this archetype, as does Dorothy in the Wizard of Oz, as she oversees the healing and transformation of her three allies. By overseeing this care, the Sovereign (Queen/King) is demonstrating their service to the world and inspires others to do the same.

But wisdom isn't just attained through thinking and feeling, you must apply the learning you gain. The Sage then helps you discern when and how to apply the wisdom from your experience. This builds self-trust as you activate your intuitive powers and capabilities.

Both Gandalf and Galadriel, the Elf Queen of Lothlorien in The Lord of the Rings, demonstrate their Sage abilities by knowing when and how to act at certain times. It is also important to note that they both experience feelings of uncertainty and doubt. There are times when they simply do not know what to do and cannot see the future outcomes of collective actions.

And finally, after going through your journey into responsibility, trust, healing, transformation, wisdom, discernment and intuition, you are ready to embrace and open yourself to joy, appreciation and spontaneity. This is the realm of the Fool. But, where you started your journey as the Naïve Fool, you complete your journey as the Wise Fool.

The Fool is possibly the most courageous, the wisest and most joy-filled of all the archetypes. The Fool can speak truth to power in a humorous way, such that it shows up hypocrisy and pomposity. This was the purpose of the Jester in medieval and renaissance times. They could challenge the egos of those in power, even Royalty, by presenting truth in a way that brought it into the open through song, storytelling or jokes. This archetype is exemplified by C3PO in Star Wars, and Bron and often Tyrion in Game of Thrones, with their witty and often ribald observations and conversations.

In Conclusion

There are a plethora of archetypes living with you in your life. Some are more dominant than others at different stages of your life. Caroline Myss for example, the popular author of Anatomy of the Spirit, refers to four survival archetypes which are primary to all people. They are the Child, the Victim, the Prostitute and the Saboteur. Robert Moore and Douglas Gillette outline four archetypes of the mature masculine: King, Warrior, Magician, Lover, in their book of the same name.

All of these are relevant in your life's journey, but most don't appear in linear order. The pattern of the Hero's Journey is more akin to a spiral, such that as you gain wisdom, you embody a different aspect of the same archetype through a new and higher perspective of yourself and the world. You therefore experience the same situation differently, bringing an opportunity for new choices and responses. You are thus serving the purpose of your journey and fulfilling your calling by bringing these higher gifts into the world, benefitting and serving all.

PART 2

THE STAGES OF THE JOURNEY

Phase 1:
Preparation And Departure

The initial stage of the Hero's Journey begins in the Hero's *Known World*. At some point, the Hero (you) receives a *Call to Adventure*, that initiates them to *Cross a Threshold*, depart this Known World and venture into the Unknown.

"This first step of the mythological journey signifies that destiny has summoned the hero and transferred his spiritual centre of gravity from within the pale of his society to a zone unknown."

**Joseph Campbell,
The Hero with a Thousand Faces**

Artist: Kevin Ma

*"We shall not cease from exploration
And the end of all our exploring
Will be to arrive where we started
And know the place for the first time."*

— from Little Gidding by T.S. Eliot

Living your Destiny

I have just reread The Alchemist by Paolo Coelho...again. It is one of my most favourite books. I think I have read it at least five times, and each time I do, it is at an important time of change and realisation in my life.

The Alchemist is a simple tale of a young man who encounters dreams and omens, and people that inspire and encourage him to take the steps necessary to achieve his life's mission and destiny. It is a tale that clearly follows the Hero's Journey template and engages the Way of the Courageous Vulnerable and the many archetypes that serve the Hero along the way.

The main character begins in his Known World, working as a shepherd in a rural landscape in southern Spain. He hears a Call to Adventure in a dream, to travel across the seas to Egypt to uncover a great treasure. He is attracted to this dream and its lure of treasure and adventure, but is also sceptical and uncomfortable about leaving his Known World. Therefore, he initially refuses this call.

After receiving a message of encouragement from a mysterious Mentor, he eventually makes the decision to leave and Crosses the Threshold to engage with his destiny. Almost immediately, after naively walking into the new world, he encounters enemies and allies as he experiences betrayal, abandonment and the loss of all his wealth. Although he thinks seriously about immediately abandoning his quest and returning to his former home, he decides to engage with this new world, respect the omens that lead him there, and follow this new path.

He quickly establishes himself within his new world, building a life of comfort, knowledge, and wealth. After some time, he awakens to a growing dissatisfaction with his new life. This is not the life outlined in his dream. Eventually, he realises he must challenge himself again, leave this life, and follow the call of his destiny, again.

Inevitably, in making this decision, he Crosses a Threshold and decides to fully commit to his path of destiny. Again, he encounters allies and enemies, and a great Mentor who leads him to open himself to his greatest gifts: those within himself, within nature and his own heart. Here he faces fear, uncertainty and death, and is challenged to completely engage with these elements. In doing so, a whole new level of awareness and appreciation opens to him.

After these ordeals, he wins a great prize. But soon after, he loses it all again, only to find that the key to his greatest reward was in the place he had started from on his journey many years ago.

As I read the story, the realisations of my own life's journey and destiny came to me. I realised that when I came to a turning point in my life, accompanying it was a point of clarity, a point of acceptance, a point of decision and a point of action.

The *clarity* comes from knowing that your destiny is *destined.* You know that you have a great purpose, and there is a pathway leading you there. There is a great sense of relief in knowing that this is so. It's just that your destiny may not look like what you thought it was, and you still don't know *how* to get there. But it is always far grander, more compassionate, simpler, more profound and more ordinary than you thought it was or wanted it to be.

The awareness, the clarity, the acceptance and the decisions often involve letting go and surrendering all your other dreams and plans. That means letting go of *all* your desires, *all* the goal setting, *all* the missions to save the world, *all* the imaginary romantic relationships and *all* the desires for wealth and fame. *All* of them must go. **All** of them.

This is what surrendering looks like. This is emptying. And this is Preparation for your eventual Initiation.

This stage may involve physical purging, relationship breakdowns, mental and emotional breakdowns or financial and career disruption.

Or it may just be a slow realisation and awakening, as if moving through a fog, or the eventual clearing of heaviness in your body, to reveal a lightness and simple appreciation of who you are and where you are right now.

But your destiny is calling. It is a movement within you, and you are going to get there. You may as well learn how to relax and be at ease with the process because it is going to happen. You are being *called*.

And, just like in The Alchemist, it is easier to follow your destiny's path if you pay attention to the signs and omens being displayed around you. This means paying attention to the *call* of your body. Is your body asking you to change your diet or exercise routine? Or perhaps change your social or work-life obligations? You will know by listening and paying attention to what your body feels at-ease with, and ill-at-ease with. And if your body begins showing signs of dis-ease, then you definitely need to pay attention.

Learning to discern 'Yes' and 'No', is an especially important part of this process of following your calling. It builds self-trust and self-responsibility and creates a pathway to your intuition.

Your calling could be moving you away from thinking about certain people or things, and away from certain activities, like political arguments, causes and courses, or endeavouring to be *right* all the time. This is the way of *the masculine* or outwardly directed activity. (Please note that the *masculine* does not refer to gender. Both men and women have masculine qualities.)

Your heart and soul could be asking you to express yourself more fully in a greater variety of ways, such as getting in touch with your feelings and sensory awareness. It could be asking you to get involved with creative or social activities. This is the way of the *feminine*, or more inwardly directed and inspired activity. (The *feminine* also does not refer to gender. Both women and men have feminine qualities.)

A lot of people have deeply repressed emotions, which they often don't know are there. Your soul wants you to access these feelings and release them *safely*, to unburden you and free up space within you for your new purpose. This is accessing the power inherent within your vulnerability. And you cannot access that power, without going through the path of vulnerability.

Or you could be passionately resisting all these underlying movements and calls. This too is part of your Journey.

And all of this is part of your journey to realise your true self; your mature and free self, which is the gift of your destiny.

Your destiny is about finding the gifts from your journey (your knowledge, wisdom, and maturity), and bringing them back into the world, back into the community, for the benefit and well-being of all. This is the meaning of service, and it is how the collective vibration is raised, and how the world is healed and changed for the better.

Once you have made the decision and taken the action to complete the Preparation stage, then, if you are listening to the signs and paying attention to the omens, the Call will arrive. Then, you begin. You enter your Journey into the new Unknown World, the path to your destiny and purpose.

The Known World

The Known World in the Hero's Journey shows us where the Hero (You) lives and works and what is normal and ordinary in their lives. This could be a comfortable and friendly community, as it was for Frodo Baggins in The Lord of the Rings and Dorothy in The Wizard of Oz. Or conversely, it could be a place of discomfort and isolation as it was for Harry Potter or Neo in The Matrix. Either way, the Hero (You) has previously established skills and knowledge which enable them to survive in their world.

The Known World is the stage from which the Hero (You) launches. It is both your starting point and the place to which you must return. It is here you acquire skills, gifts and beliefs about life and the world that serve you in this time and place. But it is also from here that you must leave. You must leave this place of familiarity and launch yourself to begin your journey.

The Known World doesn't just describe a place, like a home, a town or workplace, it also describes your familiar relationships, common tasks, ways of thinking, perceiving and behaving. In this world, you could be a high functioning and respected person like Frodo Baggins, or cynical and nihilistic like Thomas Anderson (aka Neo) in The Matrix.

In your ordinary life, your first Known World is that of your family. We all grow up in some sort of family system with various challenges, benefits and dysfunctions. Mostly, it is these issues generated through your family life, the fears, wounds and beliefs, which you must work through on your journey. These become primary motivations, both consciously and unconsciously, for the decisions you make on your journey.

For many people, their Known World (family and work situations), don't provide their basic human needs of safety and security: belonging, connection and love, power and significance, freedom and autonomy, and fun and learning.

If you grew up in a family that did not provide safety or security, this will become a major theme for you in future relationships. Many parents are controlling, and so freedom and autonomy may become major elements in your journey. For others, feelings of abandonment and lack of love from their caregivers fuel their journey and search in their lives for the 'perfect' partner or 'soul-mate'. Alternatively, they may desire or search for a surrogate family in work, community or 'tribe'.

The Known World provides the issues and challenges you must deal with, confront and then reconcile with on your journey. These are the issues you must eventually embrace and transcend. You cannot run away from them or avoid them forever. You must eventually face your issues, your pains and wounds, and deal with them. The problem for many of us though is that we mostly have very few role models who have taken that courageous course of action to show us the way.

The purpose of the Journey then is to challenge your perception of yourself and your relationship to your Known World, so much so, that you will eventually step into the process of transformation, willingly.

The difficulty of this beginning stage of the Journey is demonstrated by the often-desperate measures and rationalisations many people use to stay in their Known World, even if this means staying in deeply toxic and abusive relationships or workplaces. This stage then shows us the tenacity and perseverance of many people to stay in this world, but also the great courage they demonstrate in leaving these environments and go on their journey.

PHASE 1: PREPARATION AND DEPARTURE

Artist: Lili Popper

Stage 1:
The Call to Adventure

The Call to Adventure marks a transition from the Known to the Unknown World. The Hero (You) is introduced to their quest or vision of great consequence.

Fear of change, failure, and even death, however, often leads the Hero to *refuse* this *Call to Adventure*.

The Known World represents your comfort zone. The Unknown World signifies the journey into a land of grand possibility, but uncertain outcomes. It is the land of unmanifested dreams and potential.

The Hero resists change initially but is ultimately forced to make a critical decision: embark on the adventure and follow your *calling* or forever remain in the Known World with its sense of security and certainty, but ultimate dissatisfaction.

When Things Don't Fit Anymore

Long ago, when I was a little kid, I remember doing laps in the bathtub. I really enjoyed it. I would push off at one end, hold my breath, and flip around and around, doing laps.

Maybe I had just seen the Olympic swimmers on TV and I was trying to emulate them, I don't remember. But I remember really enjoying it. It was both an adventure and a challenge; to hold my breath and see how many times I could go around and around. I don't remember how old I was; maybe four or five years old.

But then one day, I found I couldn't do it anymore. I didn't fit anymore. I knew I was too old now and too big to do that anymore. I knew I had to let go of something I really enjoyed. I knew I wasn't a little kid anymore. I was growing up. And I was sad, and I couldn't do anything about it.

I think maybe we had gone camping over summer or visited relatives in Canberra for four or five weeks. We probably went camping down at Shoreham or Point Leo where we would go swimming and play cricket on the beach. We would get hot and salty and sandy and have showers in the smelly concrete camping ground bathroom facilities.

And when we got home, I remember so looking forward to getting in the bath and doing laps.

So, I filled the bath, got my goggles, readied myself, held my breath and pushed off. And I realised, I couldn't do it anymore. I didn't fit. I was too big now. I was too old. And I knew there wasn't anything wrong with that. There was nothing I could do. I was sad that I couldn't be that little kid anymore and do my little adventure activity anymore. I had to let go of something I really enjoyed doing.

In 2016, I saw many people passionately holding onto identities and activities that just didn't fit anymore. These were recreational activities, relationships, or even a sense of mission and purpose. Some were literally willing to push themselves to the point of death to fulfil these old identities and missions. Eventually, after receiving medical treatment, even these passionate *Warriors* had to surrender and let go of their 'mission' and allow themselves a time of rest and recovery.

These people demonstrated to me clearly that as your sense of purpose and mission kicks in, your choices naturally narrow, and you become more and more focussed in your intent and purpose. Other interests that you were once passionate about, no longer seem to fit anymore. There's nothing wrong with that. You have just outgrown that 'bathtub', so-to-speak.

But what happens when this passionately-held mission, identity and purpose, *is* the bathtub that you are growing out of? Who are you then? What is your purpose now?

This is what the process of coming to awareness and enlightenment looks like. It's very ordinary. It can be sad, it can be abrupt, and it can be lonely to leave that known and familiar way, territory or perception behind. But we don't fit that way anymore. To try to keep doing that old way, to try to fit into the too-small bathtub, will only cause ourselves and others pain and discomfort.

This is until we are willing to step out, and allow the old to fall away, realise there is nothing wrong and no-one to blame, and step into our new way and being. We are emptying and surrendering to a new way, which is yet to be revealed. This is what the completion of a soul contract looks like. It is the ending of one way of seeing and doing, and the beginning of a new path and way of being.

Now, having let go of so much over many years, I feel free as I engage with a sense of emptiness. I know I have released that which doesn't fit me anymore. It feels like I am in a place of pure potentiality, a state of creative flow and allowing. I feel grateful during these moments, even though I am uncertain of what the *next stage* looks like or when it will appear. But I know the next great stage of my life will appear, and is appearing in my life, I just don't know when or how it will show up.

And I know for sure, I cannot go back to the old bathtub. I know I don't fit there anymore.

STAGE 1: THE CALL TO ADVENTURE

Resisting the Call

Resistance is an important and natural part of your journey. Working with resistance by acknowledging it, accepting it, allowing it, and then releasing it, become the ways through. So why is it there?

Resistance can be healthy and productive, or it can be unhealthy and painful.

It can be healthy in that it enables you to create boundaries and assert your integrity. Your values assert themselves in your life and you then resist the encroachment of other people's desires and priorities upon your own.

Resistance in beginning a project or even making a decision can also show you that you are not ready or comfortable with what is being proposed or how it is unfolding. This shows that either your fear or your intuition is

guiding you to look deeper into what is going on. Part of you is saying, "no" to participating or engaging in the proposal. This is an example of how feelings in your body assist you in understanding what is going on within you and outside of you.

However, resistance can also show you that there is work to be done within you. It can show up in your life through blaming other people, avoidance behaviours, distractions, procrastination or by getting involved with causes or relationships rather than attending to what is happening right now.

And the *work* needs to be done.

One of the habits I have created for myself over the last ten years or so is noticing when I am resisting or avoiding some task or duty, and consciously allow myself to be with that feeling. I allow myself to be distracted, with full awareness, for a period.

In a relatively short time, my body gets so pissed off at **not** doing what I need to do, that I will go ahead, sit down and attend to the task anyway. Then…I just get into it. I just do it. I have just been waiting for the critical mass of energy to build up, so I can attend to the task fully.

There are also many famous procrastinators who have achieved great things. Frank Lloyd-Wright, the celebrated American architect was one such person. In late 1934, he had taken a commission from a client to design and build a great weekend home for them in rural Pennsylvania. Well, nine months went by and he had literally done nothing on the project. One morning, Lloyd-Wright received a phone call from the client who said he was coming out to Lloyd-Wright's property to see the progress made on the designs. He told the client they were progressing wonderfully well (all bullshit of course).

In the three hours that it took for Edgar Kaufman Jr, the client, to make it out to the property, Lloyd-Wright had completed designs and sketches for one of his most beautiful and iconic houses. He had designed Fallingwater (pictured).

This is to show that resistance may provide you with the time you need to become the person you need to be, to generate the energy, skills and ideas that you need to fulfil the project fully.

This natural state of being shows me that it's okay not to be perfect and pure all the time. You don't have to be *'on'*, *all* the time. To do so, can actually be counter-productive to what you are trying to achieve in your life. This also means it's okay for others not to be perfect and pure, and *'on'* all the time too.

By going through this process of acknowledging and accepting the resistance within you, you demonstrate that acceptance to others as well. And by doing so, you build greater trust, appreciation and awareness for the benefit of all.

Awakening Isn't Enough - You Must Do the Work

Most people awaken…and then they realise they must do the *work*.

The *work* being to take responsibility for who you are, where you are, and what is in your field. By 'field', I mean your auric field or energy body. That is, the planes of consciousness or energy that surround, permeate and encompass you as a human being.

The work of taking responsibility for yourself is not a little thing. It may seem simple, but just to realise that basic concepts like 'responsibility' and 'blame' are *not* the same, is a big step forward.

That is, *I* am responsible for what is in my field, but *I* am not *to blame* for it. Just coming to terms with this simple concept can be a major awakening moment and be a huge part of your life's journey.

For example, I am not personally to blame for my childhood circumstances, nor for the injustices, I may experience in my life. These are the normal workings of life and beyond my powers to control or influence them, especially as a child.

But *I am* responsible for how I respond to what happens. I am responsible for whether I harbour resentment or find ways to safely dissipate and clear unhealthful and unhelpful feelings and energies from my field.

But life, like nature, is impersonal in its workings. Your *work* in this life is not about getting everything right, or learning and reciting texts, sitting for hours in meditation, or eating the *right* diet; it *is* about taking responsibility for what is in your field. This is profound work. It is the Hero's Journey, it is the work of the courageous vulnerable, and it is the work that changes and heals the world.

This means feeling the feelings you are experiencing and allowing them to flow. You don't have to understand them or know where they came from. But you do have to do the hard work of allowing that energy to flow through you, be released and transmuted. By doing so, you create a platform of 'ease of flow' that creates the freedom which the awakening process is all about. This is both the work and reward of awakening, and it can be learnt, practiced and transmitted to others.

The Ego Is Real

We are all born with an ego and it has a job to do, just like your legs, your kidneys and your ears. But just like your legs, your kidneys and your ears, it has limitations. It is there to provide a filter on reality, so you don't get overwhelmed with the huge amount of sensory information you experience in each moment. This is occurring in all directions and dimensions all at once, from the vast spectrums of light and sound surrounding you, to your tactile environment, and the immensely complex nature of human interactions and expectations. This is a huge job to digest and make meaning from this vast potpourri of inputs you experience in each moment.

Therefore, in the early stages of growth, your ego is there to protect you and help you create boundaries and narrow your focus, so you can adapt and live more easily in this world.

Imagine you as a spirit coming into this world and trying to understand it. There is so much information and stimulus for you to interpret and process through your limited senses in each moment. All these stimulants, like noise, smells, light, radiation, foods, other people and their motivations and your own needs and desires, would completely overwhelm you if you didn't have some sort of filter system.

Hence, the ego was created to filter these inputs to a manageable level, so you can live and interact in this world, safely. But just like your kidneys and lungs, ultimately, your ego is there to serve a purpose greater than itself

STAGE 1: THE CALL TO ADVENTURE

and its narrow functioning. The ego's journey then, is to eventually humble itself to serve your greater Self and higher purpose, and not become the central focus of your life.

The ego, therefore, provides you with a layer of protection. Your beliefs, your persona, your perceptions and identity, are therefore all part of this protection mechanism.

Problems arise however, when your ego rules you. It creates an identity around your things, thoughts, beliefs, and perceptions. It can, therefore, get very selective with information, limiting your views, ensuring you feel safe and have a sense of control over yourself and your environment.

Having control, however, can narrow your focus, your attention and ability to attend to change and adapt to it in your life. This means you may judge, criticise or attack people or ideas that fall outside of your comfort zone. This is the Shadow side of the ego. It is trying to keep you safe, by keeping you in your known and normalised world.

Your ego is a powerful force, and one to befriend, and not make an enemy of. When it controls you though, you live and work from an inner belief of lack, fear, competition and righteousness. But as you go on your Journey and encounter the Road of Trials, you eventually come to the place where you must confront the realisation of your own limitations. At this point, you gain an awareness that enables your ego to serve your Higher Purpose, rather than usurping your sovereignty and becoming a tyrant. If it does so, your ego will demand that you serve it, and all its limitations, desires and need to control, rather than it serving you.

This is one of the great purposes of the Hero's Journey. It is taking you on a Journey of providing you with a sense of control, safety and mastery through your ego, and then through the path of Trials and Challenges, all of this mastery, is broken down and released. This ego-self, the small sense of self of desire, achievement and control, must die, so a greater sense of purpose and service can arise. This is the path of the Courageous Vulnerable.

Vulnerability Scares People

Vulnerability is experienced as a verb. You actually have to *do* it! It is an act of loving, and it can be very scary.

In relationships, vulnerability means you have to attend to your partner as they venture into the unknown lands of their depth. You need to hold them while they go access their inner self. You must *listen* to them, even if it triggers your own limitations. It's hard. It's tough, and it's not for most. But it *is* for some, and they are a growing population willing to go there. The world is changing. We are moving into the heart of being a true and expanded, multi-dimensional human being right now. And it is hard. It is hard to go to our depths, into our vulnerability, and uncover our wounds.

We are becoming more courageous and willing to drop our defences, shields and armour, and move into a space of vulnerability, even just for short periods. And the more we do it, the more we *can* do it. And the *more* we do it, the more others can do it too.

There are many of course who still seek the protective barriers of living in a conceptual world filled with ideology, judgements and righteousness. These qualities create separation between people, as we naturally seek out like-minded people to confirm our desire to differentiate ourselves from others.

There are also many who are unwilling to go beyond the habits of co-dependence, neediness and woundedness. They may have established power centres around their pain and fear losing control of their environment. This is how a 'pain-body' (as Eckhardt Tolle would say) thrives and survives within families: by controlling people, especially those less-powerful, and their environments.

So how do you keep yourself safe when these people are asserting their righteousness, their neediness and control? Well, stop hanging out with them! Stop arguing with them! They don't want to change. Stop trying to change them! Leave. Get out! Stop trying to *fix* everything and control your environment. Let it go and move on. You don't need to save everybody.

You cannot save everybody. And that's alright. It's ok to attend to your own needs.

Go within. Heal your own wounds. Don't just talk about it; accept the challenge and *feel* inside and move with your intuition. Your body will be your guide. Your body knows. It has an intelligence and an awareness beyond what you think. It knows what your soul wants. And your soul wants to heal. It wants to express itself, and it wants to be free. This is loving, and this is the way of the courageous and the vulnerable.

Loving is a verb! You must *do* it, not just talk about it or think about it. Loving your self is accepting your own vulnerability, and this is essential to you fully completing your journey. By going on your journey and moving into the power of your vulnerability, you emerge cleaner, stronger, and more fulfilled than ever before. This is the Way of the Courageous Vulnerable, and it does change the world.

Welcoming Your Innocence

Your Innocence is the voice inside you, that you most often don't listen to. You get caught up in doing the *right* thing. You get caught in being in relationships, having a career and creating security for yourself. You get enmeshed in causes and fears and jobs, and more causes.

And the little voice inside, the voice of the Child, will speak of abandonment.

So, you don't listen and focus on the next cause, the next course to do, the next destination, the next client, or the next trek to hike.

And the little voice is shunned.

So, she/he goes into her cave. Your Innocence feels resentment, bitterness, anger, and loneliness.

So, you don't listen.

You focus on the disasters, the injustices, the Twin-Flame, the love 'out-there', the one-right-diet, the stories about the chemical companies, and the government conspiracies. You set up boundaries to separate *us* and your *tribe*, from *them*.

Artist: Katia Honour, Talisman

And the little voice becomes a Shadow.
And you don't listen. And the Shadow becomes a power source in your life.

So now you focus on things that become vehicles for your righteousness, entitlement, neediness and victimhood; the vehicles for your ego's expression.

Now, your identity, possessions, money, and the fear of losing it all, become most important.

And now your Shadow has the power. Your Shadow has armour, weapons, and shields to engage with the world.

And still, the little voice wants to be heard, wants to be seen, wants to be known, wants acknowledgement and affirmation.

Nothing 'out there' suffices. Not for long anyway. The Shadow shows you how to be disappointed and distrustful of others. It shows you how *not* to reveal yourself, and how to maintain your armour.

Nothing suffices until *you* do. Until you break down. Until you stop for long enough, until you become still for long enough, until you allow your breath to be long enough, that you embrace yourself; *all* of yourself. This is what the little voice has been waiting for. For you to acknowledge her/him and embrace them.

She/he has been waiting, waiting all this time, for your love, your attention, your validation, your acknowledgement, and your gratitude. The embrace, the loving, tender embrace, that you have been seeking 'out there' for so long, is really the one you need from yourself. Now.

And the Inner Voice will respond. She/he will respond with "Thank you."

"Thank you", the best words you will ever hear, from the most important person in your life: You.

The Difference Between 'Trigger' and 'Cause'

I was a big fan of Abbott and Costello when I was a kid. Many of you will probably remember one of their most famous skits where a crazed-looking man assaults Lou Costello calling out, "Niagara Falls!... Slowly I turned... step by step..." The Three Stooges did their version, as did Lucille Ball on the 'Here's Lucy' show.

It demonstrates very clearly the difference between the *cause* of someone's reaction, and the event that *triggered* that reaction.

In the skit, Lou Costello is in a police cell with a rambling and dishevelled man. They get talking, and the man tells his tale of how he was jilted by his fiancé, and how he searched all across the land to find the man who stole her from him.

As he tells his tale, he gets more and more agitated. Finally, after he says the words, "Niagara Falls", he is triggered into a state of high emotion where he launches, quite unconsciously, into a full-on assault upon Lou. He re-enacts the violent scene of him confronting his usurper saying, "Slowly I turned...step by step...inch by inch...", and belts Lou a couple of times around his head and body.

Lou is just there to absorb the unconscious rantings and actions of the other man. He even inadvertently triggers the man a second time by saying, 'Well, I'm glad I didn't say, Niagara Falls', which of course, brings on another attack, "Slowly I turned...step by step...inch by inch..."

But Lou is not the *cause*. Lou did not *cause* this man's hurt or agitation. He did not *cause* the man's angry tirade, nor did he take away the man's fiancé. He may have 'triggered' the event, but he did not cause it.

The cause was within the man's own experience and reaction to his intense feelings of betrayal, hurt and woundedness. This is the expression of 'za pain-body', as Eckhart Tolle would say.

I have witnessed many people over the last few years experiencing this 'Niagara Falls'-type triggering event. It brings forth a vast tirade of righteousness, blame and abuse, directed **at** someone else. This is often done in the name of saving the planet or protecting the rights of animals, the unfairness inherent in the world, and most recently, in conspiracy theories.

In fact, I have had these attacks directed at me too. So, what's going on?

First, I know about trigger and cause, and I know that when I receive these highly emotional, blame-filled messages and verbal assaults directed **at** me, I know it's not *about* me. It's actually about them, and what they are going through. They are just completely unconscious of what they are doing and saying, and what is going on within them.

I know not to get involved in arguing about the content of their concerns, but rather to concentrate on the feeling. By talking about the feeling present within them, I bring the interaction back into the present moment. Sometimes, this brings them back into their body, and back into some level of awareness of what they are doing and *who* they are being in this moment.

By always bringing it back to the feeling, (you sound very angry, very agitated, you are yelling at me, it sounds like you are very concerned about what is happening, I hear you say you believe there are forces in the world designed to do great harm to people, etc), it will empower you, and let them know you are not being drawn into their rant and beliefs by arguing, but rather witnessing them. By being anchored in your witness-self, you create a stable and strong foundation within which you can withstand the tumult of the storm outside of you.

I also know that humour, not sarcasm, can also break the hold of this highly charged emotional reaction. It breaks the spell the wounds and 'pain-body' have upon them. It disentangles the pain-body from their consciousness. Humour shows them that this attack may be directed ***at*** you, but it is not *about* you. It helps dissipate the energy of the pain-body, ensuring it will eventually leave that person, and not get stuck on you.

This process of breaking the spell, and breaking the circuit, moves them into conscious awareness of what they are doing, saying and being right now. They become aware they are yelling and righteously arguing their beliefs. They become aware of the emotion raging through them at that moment. They become aware that what they are saying doesn't make sense. This can be both humbling and deeply embarrassing as they become consciously aware of how unconsciously they are behaving.

I also know that these unconsciously held feelings of hurt and deep-seated wounds *must* be expressed. They *must* be expressed **safely**, so they can be released. But the person carrying them is not aware enough to do so, so they launch attacks upon others who express different opinions, have different experiences, or have different awarenesses. This is how the pain-body maintains its life and energy, by projecting itself onto others. This shows that the feeling is real, but the reason behind it is not.

Often those who hold energies of light and innocence become the targets of these emotional attacks. It is the dark and shadow within someone that wants to attack or control those who hold higher vibrations of light within their presence. By controlling, blaming, or berating these people, they ensure that their own light is not awakened, it remains shut-down. This provides the perpetrator with a false sense of security and power by maintaining control over others in their environment.

This often occurs within a family, as one or both parents unconsciously project their insecurities and fears upon their children or their partner. The consequence of this over time is Wounded Child-adults. Wounded Child-adults have layers of unresolved issues which rule their relationships and interactions with the world.

But expressing these feelings outwardly *at* someone doesn't dissipate, resolve or transmute the energy long-term. It builds the defences around the wound instead. Therefore, someone can still be expressing childhood anger whilst in their 40s, 50s, 70s or older.

But these feelings must be expressed *safely*, and someone needs to witness them or hold them, so the healing process can occur. This means, as long as people have unconsciously held wounds, as unfair as it is, someone must bear the brunt of their expression.

I know many people, women and men, who have endured these attacks and assaults over many years. For many, these personal attacks have deeply affected their sense of self-worth and self-value and how they interact with the world. They believed, of course falsely, that *they* are the cause of these tirades. This is **not** true.

Thankfully, these people have survived, and have been on their healing journey, uncovering their true selves, and learning how to express themselves, safely.

I hail the courage of such people. Thank you for your work in enduring the 'slings and arrows of outrageous fortune' to help heal the world.

The Creative and Destructive Power of Emotion

The creative and destructive power of emotion is like a wave coming into shore. It begins as a swell line far out to sea. Just a line on the horizon that slowly gains definition as it rolls along. Then, as it comes closer to shore, it slows down, builds up power and concentrates its force into a peak. This force gathers up the water before it, building up its power even further, and then finally it breaks and surges forth onto the shore. This power, now expended, recedes into the ocean itself, becoming one with its source again.

This process of wave formation and dissolution mirrors the triggering of emotional outbursts. Most people, however, even *spiritual* and *aware* people, confuse 'trigger' and 'cause'.

When triggered by something, you may direct your pent-up emotional destructiveness *at* someone, rather than feeling the emotion all the way through yourself. If instead of directing this highly-charged energy *at* someone (such as, blaming, accusing or condemning them), you allow yourself to feel the emotion (the anger, fear, anxiety, or resentment), you then become the catalyst of its transformation. You transform all that energy through your body, as uncomfortable as it is, into more creative and flowing energy.

You allow the energy to form into a wave, crash through you, and inevitably, to wash upon the shore and go back into the ocean, back to the greater source of all energy.

This is a way of loving yourself by respecting whatever it is you are feeling in the moment. This is also respecting the lives and energies of others around you, by not directing this powerful and destructive force out *at* them. By doing so, you build greater trust, power and harmony, within yourself, and within the world.

Fear is Real

Fear is real. We really feel fear. It is a tremendously powerful emotion and energy. It distorts our sight and perception, narrows our thinking and capacity to take action. The cause of our fear, however, is mostly not real. They are the monsters in the cupboard and the scary things under the bed, and the enemies outside our door.

The challenge is to experience the fear and allow it to flow through your body, but understand that the cause you associate with it, the meaning you give to it, is often imaginary. Your explanations for your feelings of fear and anxiety are mostly not real and not true.

Enlightenment comes to you as you realise that the foundational beliefs you have about yourself and the world, such as, 'I am not good enough', 'it was because of me', 'I am not lovable', or 'I'm dumb', are not true. But the underlying feeling these beliefs are expressing unsafety, fear, and abandonment and not being good enough, are real and are true. It is the journey to uncover these unconsciously held underlying feelings, and allow them to be transmuted, that is the pathway into your vulnerability, your courage and your freedom.

Your compassion and awareness are then expressed by acknowledging the feeling and providing a means for it to move through your body and leave. This is demonstrating love to the one who holds that feeling: You. This is the process of healing and making yourself whole, and this is real. This is the way of the courageous vulnerable, and it is practiced in your daily life.

Making a Decision...Trusting Your Intuition

Some say making a decision is about discerning the difference between your head and your heart. It is said that if the decision is calculated and made with an understanding of risk, then it is of the head, and if that decision is based in *passion*, *wildness* or *bliss*, this is of the heart. Many in the spiritual and self-development communities suggest that to live from your heart is the best way to live. "Follow your passions," they say. Yet often, even these heart-felt, passionately made decisions, goals and dreams, don't turn out well either.

Another approach is listening to your intuition, and making decisions and taking action from there. This means practising the discipline of stillness and listening. You must be able to discern the difference between the movement of your thoughts and emotions, and those feelings you have from an intuitive sense. By doing so, you build self-trust and awareness.

This intuitive sense is *knowing*. It is a still point within a swirling vortex of emotions (desire, fear, anger, lust, infatuation, righteousness, anxiety and getting it right), and thoughts of the future (relationships, money, career, and purpose, etc.). This knowing comes in the form of words or images or senses that have no emotion attached to them. It just says, "call him", "go there", "say this", or "do this action". They are simple words or phrases, or just an impulse to action or awareness. This *knowing*, this stillness and sense, is what 'Yes' looks like.

Illustrating this, in 2016 I was sitting quietly in my room watching a movie, when I received an intuitive knowing. "Create", it said. That's it. That's all. "Create what?", I asked, knowing full well that I wouldn't get any further response and that I had all the information I needed. So, I tossed around a few ideas as to what I could do, writing, drawing, singing, or making a collage. And I got started.

I collected old magazines, advertising pamphlets and new-age newspapers and proceeded to cut out interesting pictures, images, words and phrases. I then put them together in interesting ways as a collage and stuck them onto pieces of butcher's paper. I was creating. I was fulfilling the directive of my intuition.

After about six weeks or so, I had created about ten pieces which contained thoughtful and visually interesting representations of my beliefs, values and desires. They were colourful pieces that expressed my sincere desire for community, health and healing, an affinity with powerful landscapes and the Australian environment, for fun and expression, and for a sanctuary enabling deep level transformation and growth.

I enjoyed reviewing them, placing them around my bedroom, and looking at how they could become a future life. However, suddenly, another intuitive knowing came to me. "Burn it", it said. That's it. That's all. I shrugged my shoulders and said, "Okay". So the following day, at the height of the full moon, I went outside to the fire pit in the backyard, and ceremonially, burnt my creations. It was an act of letting go, and I felt fine. I wasn't losing anything, but rather gaining a sense of purpose and expansion.

For me, the purpose of this exercise was not just about following my intuition, but to show me not to be attached and defined by the images I had created. I felt like the lesson was much like that of the Tibetan monks who would, as a community, make beautifully coloured and intricately designed sand mandalas over a week or so, and then, ritualistically, destroy them all.

This exercise illustrates how your intuition is not a 'high-five' moment of passion and exaltation, but rather a sense of clarity and knowing. There is a sense of ease and timelessness; everything is alright. You just *know* what you need to do. You *know* the steps that take you further along the path. It doesn't mean that everything will work out smoothly, it just means that at this moment, you are aligned with your Soul and you are listening and paying attention.

You also know that this may mean leaving certainties behind. You could be very afraid when making this choice. You don't know what the outcome will be because you are making a decision that may not seem rational or calculated.

And sometimes this choice means...waiting, doing nothing, just waiting for the tide to come in, rather than chasing the dream and launching your boats before everything is ready. This is the painful side of our action-oriented, 'Just-Do-It' culture, that 'doing nothing' is not considered a valid or valuable action.

Listening to my intuitive voice has often meant taking action that is exactly the opposite of what I wanted and what is comfortable. Many of these decisions have turned out badly too and have not brought about greater peace or well-being. I realise now, I was probably still listening to the voice of my fear and hope and then taking action, rather than sitting in stillness and waiting.

I am aware now, there were many times I was consumed with anxiety and the necessity to act, leading to times of great stress and pressure. The correct action may not have been to leave that job or shun that relationship, but to stay and continue engaging with my feeling. The right action would have presented itself eventually, and I would have been more trusting and stable when I needed to act.

However, because of the great changes in the world, now is the time to make decisions based in intuition and the call of the Soul. This is one of the great lessons and practices of the Hero's Journey: trusting your Self. This is enacting courage in your ordinary life. This is the practice of opening yourself to your vulnerability and discovering what lies within.

Just knowing this doesn't mean you will manifest what you desire. It does mean, however, that you are acting in accordance with your soul's guidance, and you are becoming that which you were always meant to be.

The Universe *is* always working for you, not just to get you what you want (the narrow and popular interpretation of the 'Law of Attraction' and Manifestation), but to bring you into the greatest and highest version of yourself. And most people don't know who or what that is, and paradoxically, you are not supposed to.

To discover and uncover this reality requires your Journey into humility and this is the way of the *Courageous Vulnerable*. This is the true meaning of manifestation; attracting the circumstances and materials you need to live out your highest soul purpose in this lifetime.

Not Knowing Everything is Alright

I remember as I was growing up, in my teens, I started noticing that a *lot* of people knew *everything*. They knew the motivations of others, could identify what's wrong with other people, or what's wrong in history or the government, or with the wider world. They knew **everything**! They had all the answers to everything, and I knew, in contrast, that I didn't. I knew I *didn't* know.

I was intimidated by these people. I was intimidated by their certainty and absolute sense of knowing. It brought into stark contrast my absolute sense of uncertainty, self-doubt and unknowing.

At that time, I knew I was uncertain about myself. I had big self-doubts and wasn't sure about what I believed in, what I wanted, what sort of career awaited me, what I was good at, or how I was going to survive in the world. I knew though, I was uncertain, and I knew I was afraid. And I knew I had to hide that knowing.

Occasionally, some people would disparage me for being vague as I couldn't make decisions quickly or easily at that time. There seemed to be a fog in my mind so I couldn't see or understand issues quickly or easily. I knew I was uncertain about so many things. I didn't even know if I was safe. Actually, I did know that. I knew I didn't feel safe in my environment, at home or at school.

But later, in my 20s, I realised that those people who knew *everything*, really didn't. They really didn't know everything at all. They just *thought* they knew everything. They just believed they knew everything. They would loudly say, with absolute confidence, that they *know* this or that thing is true! And they believed it with absolute conviction. But mostly, what they believed in was not true. It just wasn't true.

I realised that they just wanted to be right. It feels good to be right and to make others wrong. That certainty brings a sense of power, safety and confidence. So, they found ways to prove themselves right. This was the emanation of their ego in their lives. They expressed a worldview and sense of self based in limitation, comparison, and separation.

I have listened to many people who are certain about so many things: God, immigration, the-one-right-diet, the correct spiritual practice, corrupt politicians, the environment or Big Pharma and the 5G terror. But I've always known that there was something else going on. There was something more. Even when I was a kid, even then, I knew that life and the world were way more complex than the simplistic, black-and-white, righteous worldviews expressed by some.

Myth, Paradox and Mystery

I suppose this was one of the reasons why I liked the Greek and Roman myths and legends books I read so avidly as a kid. 'The Dreamtime Book' by

STAGE 1: THE CALL TO ADVENTURE

Artist: Ainslie Roberts – Songman and the Two Suns

Charles Mountford, with amazing paintings by Ainslie Roberts, was one of my absolute favourites.

These stories highlighted the complexity and often unfairness of the way of the world. They told stories of gods and spirits who would often behave in impetuous ways that were totally unfair to the folk in the tales. The Aboriginal stories in the book The Dreamtime, gave me my first awareness of the reality of the aliveness of the landscape and the spirit-world of Australia. And of this, I was certain. I knew that the land of

Australia was alive and filled with spirit. That was absolute. I felt it and I knew it. It is true.

And the paintings. Oh... the paintings by Ainslie Roberts truly brought me into the landscape; the mystery, the energy, and the surreal nature inherent in the stories. I was drawn into the mystery of it all, and I knew, absolutely, that the mystery was real. The mystery was the one true and absolute certainty in life.

And the people who know everything... they have no sense of mystery. They are mystified by the paradox presented by mystery; that there is certainty within the uncertainty. For them, everything must be circumscribed and defined. It is a literal, linear, binary and material experience of the world, and nothing else. That's it. It's either *this* or *that*. But I know that that is not the way the world works. It is not literal, it is not linear, and it is absolutely not binary. Life and the world are so much more spectacular and multi-dimensional than that. Even quantum physics tells us this.

I'm now ok with people who think they know *everything*. I don't feel intimidated by their certainty anymore. I know they really don't know, and they too are on a journey into the mysteries of life. I'm also now ok with challenging their views, and even copping the anger and sometimes abuse that comes when that point of cognitive dissonance hits the fan. I know that knowing everything isn't enough. It takes much more than that to engage fully with life and our journey within it.

And one thing I have always known for certain, that life and the world are a mystery, with simple complexities and paradoxes inherent within it. And I feel safe and secure in my certainty of that.

Mentors, Helpers and Guides

During your Hero's Journey, you will meet with mentors, helpers and guides. In movies, you see Obi Wan Kenobi mentoring Luke Skywalker in Star Wars. In The Matrix, Morpheus mentors Neo, and in The Wizard of Oz, Glinda the Good Witch guides Dorothy, as well as having helpers like the Lion, the Tin Man and the Scarecrow.

STAGE 1: THE CALL TO ADVENTURE

But in your ordinary life, these mentors and helpers may just be a friend, a colleague, a lover, or perhaps just some ordinary Joe you meet on the bus. Their job is to provide you with information or stimulus that leads you on your journey to your future self. Whether they know it or not, they are there to provide the impetus; words, circumstances, or conditions, for you to 'wake up' out of your normal, familiar mindset and into a *new* way of seeing and being. This is how the ordinary people around us, are part of our journey to fulfil our purpose in life.

This journey into the *new* can sometimes involve going through hellish circumstances and transitions. This is where the old and familiar ways, which were sometimes highly successful, don't work anymore. Your ego, which is there to keep you safe, will often argue and defend the old ways, even if it leads to attacking or rejecting the help you need. This means that at times, you must walk alone, sometimes surrounded by darkness, until you are finally humbled and cry out again for assistance.

This is an incredibly challenging stage. Your mentor and helpers, and your circumstances, are all challenging your perceptions and the way you work in the world. It is challenging because for many of you, especially those who grew up with an inferior sense of self, accepting the reality of the power and wisdom that is inherent within you, can be intensely stressful and even overwhelming. This realisation of your true power and magnificence challenges your view of yourself profoundly.

These mentors, therefore, aren't always there just to be nice and lovey-dovey, leading you to some magic Nirvana (as much as you would love it to be so). They are there to lead you to the Force (in Star Wars), the Source (in The Matrix), or qualities of heart, courage and wisdom which lie within you (in The Wizard of Oz). And delivering harsh love to you, through words of truth that force you to accept responsibility and your current reality, may be one of their methods to get you there.

But this is the brilliance of the journey you are on: realising the truth of the light inherently within you, and walking with others, as you ever so reluctantly, integrate this light into your life.

Saving the World

I saw a friend recently who complimented me on my health.

"Thanks", I said. "I've become a Vague-an".

"A Vague-an?", she asked, "What's a Vague-an? Don't you mean Vegan?"

"No, no, Vague-an", I said. "That's where I'm not quite sure what I'm eating or why, but I am absolutely certain everybody else should feel guilty and ashamed for not doing the same."

Vague-an - Saving the world, in a definitely roundabout kinda way.

Meditation with School Children – Becoming A Mentor

I just completed a two and half minute meditation/visualisation with Preps and Grade Ones (five and six-year-olds). It's a very simple process: the breath comes in and goes out, we count to four on the in-breaths, and count to six on the out-breaths. A golden ball is visualised moving down through the body, into the earth and back up again through the body, bringing strength, clarity and power.

After this, I ask, "Does anyone feel different now than what you did before?". In response, these answers stood out:

A grade one girl said her growing pains had stopped. "Where in your body is that?" I asked. "In my knee, my foot and my leg", she replied.

"My neck feels happy", said one boy who sometimes gets migraines. And another boy said he "felt connected with everything."

Little kids eh! Love it!

At another school, I did some mindfulness meditation with nine to eleven-year-olds. They had never done meditation before, so it was a completely new experience for them. Their feedback too was revealing and amazing.

I followed the same process of meditation and questions. Some of the responses were, "I could feel the smartness coming into me", "It felt like I was in a cloud", "I felt like I was invincible", "I felt like I was beyond Pluto." And one boy said, "I felt like I was released from a jail I had been in my whole life", Wow! That was a powerful experience.

Similarly, another boy said, "This may sound strange to you, but it's not strange to me. Before I felt like an idiot, and now I don't feel like an idiot." Whoa!, I thought to myself, that's a **big** one!

Finding ways for children to experience the reality of their inner world through meditation is a simple and profound way of expanding their experience and awareness. It's wonderful to provide this opportunity for them.

Artist: Steve de la Mare

It is also a way in which I become a mentor and guide for them in their lives too. They then are benefitting from my experience and my willingness to share this knowledge and process with them. This is how wisdom is passed on, and I am grateful for the opportunity to do so.

Questions and Exercises:

1. Give some thought as to when, where and how this first stage of the Hero's Journey has appeared in your life.
   - Describe the Known Worlds you have experienced in your life. Name three of them. Eg: your family life, your workplace, even your belief systems.
   - What were the gifts and pressures within these worlds?
   - What archetypes were most dominant for you in your Known World? Eg: the Mother, the Victim, the Bully, the Nature Child, the Pioneer, etc?
2. When and how did you receive your 'Call to Adventure'?
   - How did it show up in your life? Eg: a job offer, a new relationship, an adventure holiday, etc?
   - What pressures presented to you to leave? What pressures presented to you to stay?
   - How did you make your decision to go or stay?
3. When, where and how has a mentor appeared in your life? Name three of these occasions.
4. What were the gifts and the pressures this Mentor brought to you? (Please note: a mentor isn't always benevolent like Dumbledore or Mary Poppins, they can also be harmful.)
5. Name three things from the first part of the book that moved you or struck you as important.
6. Creative expression - drawing: Find a quiet space. Breathe deeply and relax your body. Feel the breath go all the way through your body and clear your mind. With paper, coloured pencils or crayons in front of you, ask yourself clearly, "Show me what is important for me to know from this part of the book."

   Then, with your non-dominant hand, choose a pencil or crayon, and start drawing. It doesn't matter what it looks like, just create. Change hands when your body tells you. Repeat.

Stage 2:
Crossing the Threshold

This stage marks the place of a major life-changing decision. It is a turning point. The call has been heard, doubts and fears have been expressed, and preparations have been made.

From here, the Hero (You) commits to the path of walking into the Unknown. Sometimes this decision is made willingly and joyfully with the blessing and welcome advice from mentors and guides. Other times, events outside of your control, plunge you into this path.

And once the threshold has been crossed, the Hero cannot return until they have completed their Journey and fulfilled their quest. If they return too early, having not uncovered their gifts and boons, there are dire consequences. There is no turning back, at least, not by the way you came.

Artist: Hartwigg Kopp Delaney

Crossing the Threshold

Crossing-the-threshold of the Known into the Unknown world is a big deal. It can be wrenching as you weigh up loyalties to yourself and your priorities, and to those people and circumstances that keep you back in the Known world. These could be family, relationships, career, a house, or other obligations. It could even be the world of addiction, self-sabotage and co-dependence.

But there comes a moment of quietude where you get a chance to review and contemplate the wide expanse of *what could be*. You may visualise the Unknown World and all its possibilities and your potential within it. You can see it. It is now a less scary place, and entering it seems more possible as the fear and anxiety that clouds your judgement moves away to reveal the likely steps ahead. You can see yourself living and succeeding in this new world.

This is not about 'following your bliss' (an oft-quoted adage from Joseph Campbell), but rather noticing and listening to your calling. If your calling says that you must move, then you **must** move. If you do not, and you stay back in the same circumstances, there can be grave consequences, as your internal voice and sense of self is contradicting the choices you are making in your life. Quite naturally, this creates internal pressure and conflict, which must be released somehow. This means you may either betray yourself, or those around you. Hence, you feel viscerally the dilemma, and the power of your choice to Cross the Threshold into the Unknown World.

"Do what you can, with what you have, where you are."
Theodore Roosevelt

Many people experience the desire to 'get out of the rat race' and establish their own business which they hope will give them financial, emotional and spiritual freedom, as well as the fulfilment of a grand sense of purpose. But what if the 'dream' doesn't eventuate? How then does a job help you achieve the dream you want? Isn't this the opposite of freedom and fulfilling your purpose and calling?

A friend made a post on social media reflecting this question:

"My relationship to being an employee over the years has generally been one of recalcitrant dread overlaid by a strong sense of duty. A combination

of big dreams, finely tuned emotional sensitivity and authority issues has always made working for other people extremely challenging; it was always a 'stop-gap' on the way to the freedom of self-employment."

She spoke of the challenges she had endured, of colleagues, customers, and a habit of 'escaping' the pressure by flying the coop: *"...yearning for the freedom to stretch my wings and breathe."*

However, she stayed, and she committed to the unfamiliar role of employee:

"I committed to being taken into unknown waters and I discovered that, actually, I had bigger wings and that this job was holding me while I grew into them."

These "unknown waters" carried her into a place where she uncovered long-held issues with managing time, authority, communicating with management, communicating with her much younger colleagues, and of course, her relationship with money; all essential elements to master if you are to establish your own sustainable business.

For example, her issues with authority, *"...called me into digging deeper to claim my inner authority on a totally new level.... I have stood my ground and shown my anger openly to management when I have felt unsupported and unfairly treated, and discovered how ballsy I really am."*

This is where the 'rubber' of all the personal development and spiritual growth courses, all the books and meditations, 'hits the road'. It is the *ordinary world* that challenges us, and it is in the ordinary world that we must put the change into action. So, as my friend says, *"...thankfully, with a bit of help, I had the tools to feel it, heal it and move into a more expanded and powerfully effective way of being - both personally and professionally."*

My friend's story demonstrates the nobility of the ordinary. The 'Hero' in this case isn't heading off to fight in a battle or a cause, or to create a 'visionary' service or business which will heal the world. Rather the hero is an ordinary person, engaging her heart and mind and humbling herself to do something she has resisted for so long. In doing so, she engages more skills, more power, and more value than she knew she was capable of before.

She got a job in the career she had originally trained for and found a way to live fully, even though it wasn't what she wanted to do. She showed courage by engaging with her ordinary experience, staying open to the opportunities of her journey, and having a willingness to humble herself and find the power in her vulnerability. Interestingly, the word 'courage' derives from an old French word 'corage', meaning 'heart.' She was, therefore, living from the heart in the ordinary world.

As she says about her experience,

"These have been extraordinary gifts of wholeness and healing, amongst many others. I cherish what this job continues to show me. I just wanted to take a moment to acknowledge the humble day job, and all the ways it prepares the fertile ground for our soul offerings! Hail to the humble day job!"

Hail indeed. Hail the nobility of the ordinary.

Resisting and Crossing the Threshold Anyway

Crossing the Threshold - It is the beginning of a new stage in your life. It is crossing a boundary which you previously thought you couldn't or wouldn't cross. This decision draws you on a journey into an unknown world with different rules and limitations, leading to a path that uncovers your inherent gifts and talents, and your eventual transformation.

But, does a caterpillar know it will become a butterfly? Probably not, yet that is its destiny. A caterpillar will set aside a time and place where it will undergo a massive process of transformation. This metamorphosis is not a simple or romantic process, but rather one that involves the complete dissolution of a previous body and the materialisation of something completely new.

Many people go through great distress during this natural human process of transformation and evolvement. They may, quite unconsciously, try to stay as a caterpillar whilst going through the process of becoming a butterfly. Of course, in their minds they don't see themselves as caterpillars (very unsexy), but rather as Lions, or Warriors, or Goddesses or 'badasses' and revolutionaries. But they are, never-the-less, going through the process of change anyway, and becoming someone they never imagined.

Crossing the Threshold is a profound moment of decision, or it may just be as ordinary as choosing a different meal, changing your communication style, or consciously listening to someone rather than arguing with them.

But the profound part of the journey is in the transformation. This could be uncovering false foundational beliefs such as, "I'm not good enough", "It was my fault", "I'm ugly", or "There's something wrong with me". These false beliefs become foundational structures for many people, myself included. This structure is protected by defensive mechanisms and identities to shield us. We enact these shields through avoidance strategies like working too much, being funny, eating, goal setting, exercising, etc. Or we armour ourselves by being cold, cynical, belligerent, sarcastic or aggressive.

But eventually, as you go through metamorphosis and evolution, these beliefs, shields and armour must be exposed as false, and thereby breakdown. This brings forth a new, more healthful and fulfilling structure created in its place.

And just as the caterpillar becomes a butterfly, the human process of transformation must include stages of uncertainty as the previous form dissolves and the new and more beautiful embodiment is in the process of creation. Yet, even as the caterpillar literally digests itself and lives in an amorphous soup for a period, all the ingredients needed for its final incarnation as a butterfly are being activated.

So too with your human development. You need time and appropriate space for your transformation and development. And you must Cross a Threshold to get there. This may mean finding time to be by yourself, or seek healing agents, or enrol in transformative energetic programs. However it is done, the ingredients needed for your metamorphosis are within you. You just need the time, the intention and a supportive space to do so.

It is also heartening to know that the new form we transform into, is always more evolved than the old. The new being that emerges, is always more sophisticated and more capable of handling more complexity than the previous incarnation.

And so, resist as you may, if it is your destiny to become someone greater than who you are now, you will be presented with the challenge of Crossing the Threshold into a new world to do so. This challenge will present itself again and again, until you wake up, and choose to walk into your true-life path, activating your greatest talents, wisdom and power.

Mercury is Retrograde...Again

Mercury is retrograde...again...Uhhhhh!
Doesn't it do anything else?
Why can't it upgrade? Go high grade, multi-grade, get into a new grade, even go low grade for a while?
But no...it has it to be cool and go retro...pfffft.
Everyone is upgrading now. Why can't Mercury upgrade too? Like, get a new iPhone or a new Samsung...hmmm?
Or perhaps go travelling. Go to Belgrade, Leningrade or Stalingrade.
Hell, why doesn't it go all eco-friendly and just bio-degrade?
Boy oh boy...
I mean, retro? What, is it going to be out wearing corduroy pants soon, with wide shoulder pads? pffft...
Mercury, you gotta start getting with the program here buddy. Retro may be cool sometimes...I mean Ray-Bans and 1940s-style suits are always cool, but to have this as part of your identity...man...we gotta talk.
Everybody else is getting out of the Old and into the New...and you Mercury, (yer stupid bastard) always gotta go back to the Old ways ...back into your cave to go retrograde...
Buddy, it's time. R U Ok?

Endings and Beginnings...Releasing Old Ways

There are times on your Journey, that progress happens despite your efforts to stay in the old and familiar patterns and paradigms.

It's like you are moving through primary school, high school and university, and *all* your books, accomplishments, certificates and achievements, are being thrown out of your storage units and cupboards, off your mantlepiece, and out of your hidden basement. This creates an open space within your psyche and energetic field, so a grander, more complex version of you can emerge.

This is happening, despite your efforts to hang onto the old, despite your grief and lashing out at others at losing your cherished stuff. Even your woundedness and sense of injustice is leaving you. *"Ohhhh no!"*, you exclaim, *"Who am I now?"*

All this stuff, even your absolute certainties of identity and purpose, are leaving. They are leaving because you don't need them anymore. These things, beliefs and ways of being all served their purpose in the past. They helped you progress for a period, but now it is time to move on. They don't fit you anymore. They don't fit the *new* person you are becoming.

Consequently, you don't carry your grade five textbooks into high school, nor your grade ten workbooks into university. You have embodied that learning and can now discard those books. You don't need to carry them forth into your new, more complex incarnation and purpose.

On an emotional and energetic level, you also don't need to carry the wounds of your childhood and the subsequent blaming, waves of anger, depression and fear anymore. You have done the work. You have survived, experienced all of that, and now you can move on.

I was reminded the other day of the great Buddhist parable about the raft and the river. That is, a raft is a safe and useful vessel to cross a river, but not very helpful if you carry it with you on your journey up a mountain.

So 'the raft' here are the old ways of thinking, perceiving and believing. They could be your defence mechanisms and strategies, such as your armour and methods of avoidance. These may have worked in previous roles and relationships. They may have become habits embodied in a business role or vocation, such as teaching, healing or coaching. Goal setting or achievement strategies, that were once successful, won't work anymore or have the attraction power they once did. You are leaving those behind, and new, more complex ways of being in the world need to be adopted.

This 'raft' of safe and reliable ways applies in relationships of all sorts too. So, the romantic fantasies of the 'Twin Flame' movement are being left behind, as are the perfectionist expectations of partners, others and yourself. These methods of avoidance, of bypassing feelings of discomfort and not taking responsibility, are leaving.

But responsibility is an essential element of the Hero's Journey. It is where the Hero (You) shows courage by allowing yourself to accept accountability for who you are, where you are, and who you have been. This is a tough process, but when faced with honesty, it opens you to greater capabilities by bringing about greater self-trust and self-appreciation.

It is like you are moving toward your greater destiny, and you are caught in a 'tractor beam' (Star Wars reference), taking you on a journey to a destination far beyond what you could possibly have imagined, becoming a being of far greater power, wisdom and substance than you could possibly know.

But moving beyond this 'raft' of comfort is part of your Hero's Journey, and you must climb the mountain in order to see the vision of your destiny, and discover who you truly are. It is so much easier if you are not carrying the weight of the raft of unnecessary burdens like your woundedness and armour, which are very heavy indeed. Once released, the path forward is so much easier, filled with ease, flow and relief. This is the power and freedom you gain from walking into and through your vulnerability; the vulnerability to leave behind that which does not serve you anymore.

STAGE 2: CROSSING THE THRESHOLD

Artist: Steve de la Mare

We are Emerging

We are emerging from the earth,
Now.
Our heads have been filled
With so many thoughts,
So many 'shoulds',
So many righteous causes,
So much hurt and woundedness,
That we couldn't hear.
We couldn't hear the Call.
The Call to listen,
Instead of speaking.
The Call to sitting,
Instead of going.
The Call to being,
Instead of doing.
We are emerging.
We are growing.
We are becoming.
More than we ever thought.
And we are
Always
Loving.

Renouncing Old Vows and Beliefs

Your Journey becomes easier for you once you release the burdens of old beliefs, wounds and defences. One such method of relief is renouncing old vows that don't serve you anymore. This means renouncing vows that you have held either consciously or unconsciously, such as vows of poverty, addiction, being a monk, priest, or nun, vows of chastity, being 'good', or generational, inter-generational or even past-life issues.

It could mean renouncing vows that stipulated that you cannot feel good about yourself or the world until **all** people are healed, **all** injustice is resolved, **all** sickness is cured, **all** environmental issues are solved, and **all** poverty is eliminated. These are hard vows to live up to. Practically impossible. So, are they helpful anymore? Do they serve you anymore?

Ridding yourself of untrue beliefs is also a major soul contract to fulfil. Commonly held untrue beliefs are: I am not loved, I am not lovable, I'm dumb, I'm not good enough, it was my fault, I don't deserve it, I am not worthy, my mother/father doesn't love me, I am ugly, etc.

By engaging in the process of healing, you are calling upon both the Destroyer and the Creator in your life. The Destroyer engages the courage you need to deal with the defensive structures you have in place to keep you feeling safe. These could be denial, avoidance patterns like blaming or substance-abuse, defensiveness or patterns of addiction. Its purpose is often to devastate you so much that you do not have the strength to hold onto those old beliefs anymore.

You don't need to carry these unhelpful vows, beliefs and energetic systems with you anymore. It's time to let them go. They were made from places of obligation, guilt or shame, long, long ago, in childhood, or in a past life. And they serve no purpose for you anymore.

So, I hereby release these old, unhelpful vows, agreements, contracts, chords, imprints and attachments from all aspects of my mind, body and energetic fields, for the betterment and well-being of all. As I AM now. And so, it is. I AM the Light, the Light I Am.

In doing so, in releasing these old energetic systems based in fear and obligation, I release myself from burdens I do not need to carry anymore. I free myself of their weight and allow myself to walk more freely and truly in the world now. This is the power of vulnerability, and I choose to access it now.

Your soul knows your life's purpose better than you do. There's a reason for that.

"Let go or be dragged!"

The Hero's Journey takes us on paths leading to our fulfilment and ascension. And there are issues, contracts, and experiences we must go through and reconcile with to complete this path. We must Cross the Threshold and go on our journey, and we cannot take those old issues and old burdens with us. So, "Let go, or be dragged!"

Many people choose to be dragged by hanging onto old ways of thinking, beliefs and identity. They stay in relationships or jobs that are unhealthy, abusive, or even toxic. They may have a very unhealthy attitude and relationship with themselves.

Many though, have moved through relationships or jobs or unforgiveness onto paths of expansion and creativity. They have chosen to attend to their issues and achieve the freedom that comes from releasing old energy, patterns and behaviours that are not useful anymore. They are changing the underlying structure of their lives.

Others must be dragged along this path. Moving into the unknown, even if it promises relief from current pain and toxicity, is so discomforting that they will sabotage all efforts to move onto a more creative path. This is where life and the Universe has an intelligence beyond what you know. And this is a good thing.

Your Journey will present Trials and Challenges so those old patterns of fear and woundedness will be triggered and exposed. This happens so they can be acknowledged, felt, healed, and thereby transmuted. There is nothing wrong with this, even though it will sometimes be very uncomfortable.

Either way, you're going to get there. The outcome is assured. You *are* becoming all that you are meant to be. And that is a good thing.

The Journey into Growth - Leaving Home

Many people are going through a great journey into self-discovery and healing right now. It is a process of readying to Cross a Threshold and step into a new and challenging stage of growth and being.

Many people are therefore completing the first stage, the Preparation of their Hero's Journey. They are becoming aware of themselves and their current environment and its limitations. So, many are training in spiritual and energetic ways of thinking, doing and being. Many are undergoing healing at deep levels. They are preparing goals and dreams for a new way of working and interacting with the world. And, when they know the time is right, they take the first step, they Cross the Threshold and immerse themselves in this new journey.

But of course, life has its own plans for us, and I'll get to that later.

The first part of the journey sees you venturing forth towards your desired goals and dreams. You align yourself with like-minded people and use your intelligence, your determination, and your heart to establish a direction and success strategies within this new territory.

For some people, this may mean beginning a new relationship, a new career, moving to a new location, learning a new skill or way of thinking, or simply endeavouring to live a healthy life. Some people may choose to define themselves according to these new elements: for example, 'I am a Healer', 'I am a Vegetarian (or insert diet here)', 'I am a Warrior', or a 'Goddess'. Others may choose to define themselves according to things they do, like, 'I do Tai Chi/Qi Gong/Meditation', 'I do Yoga', 'I am an environmental/social activist', etc.

This stage is helping you create an identity and sense of purpose within this new world. It is a stage in which your ego and your mind are activated as they look for and find their new purpose and way of being in this environment.

It is a stage where you may also define yourself by who you are *not*, who you are against, or who you are fighting. You may then judge others who do not measure up to your ideals and expectations. And mostly, this is done quite unconsciously. This is where the Orphan and Rebel archetypes come to the fore, as you gravitate to a new 'tribe' of like-minded people.

However, as the picture illustrates, this journey occurs within a limited environment where your goals and dreams are actually illusory. Waking up to this reality can often be traumatic and can lead to a sense of distress and isolation. "How can all that I have worked for, studied and believed in for so long, be wrong?"

However, the picture shows us more. It depicts a child, a boy, who is venturing forth. A child with desires for a bright and golden future, an Innocent who lacks depth and complexity, who wants to achieve Heroic goals, to find his or her place in the world by fighting 'enemies and monsters', and those who do not believe, and by saving the world. He has faith and hope and trust, and has a fully prepared backpack, and is certain about his goal and how to achieve it: through fighting, reacting and responding.

The child in the image is tied by a cord to the central structure of his parents' house. He is tied securely to the beam in the house which runs through the upper levels and connects to its foundations. You only see a part of this structure; the bulk of it is completely hidden from view. It is in the dark, covered over by other elements, seen and unseen. He is tied, quite unconsciously, to his childhood home and the baggage and woundedness that resides there.

The picture shows us that however passionately and determinedly we go forth into our next stage, we must eventually deal with this cord, tied directly to our family of origin. It shows us that even as we look 'out there' for our sense of purpose, we will inevitably be drawn back to reconcile with this central pillar of our identity; our family.

It also shows us that as much as we believe we may be forging a new *awakened* and *enlightened* path 'out there', we are just creating a world with new rules and regulations to live by within a limited, conceptual and illusory world. For example, many people desire to eat the 'right' diet, do the 'right' spiritual practices, and exercise the 'right' way. This means they are still living within the same old structure of a parental world view. That is, if you are good and get everything *right*, and control your environment, you will be safe, praised and rewarded.

Of course, this is still living within a restricted environment, in the attic (ie, your head, concepts and beliefs), where the only view is an imaginary one. No wonder people have a hard time maturing and evolving. This is **big** stuff to come to terms with. It involves cutting the cord to the old structure, the old identity and patterns of safe-seeking and familiarity, and stepping into a completely new and uncertain structure and pattern. But the outcomes from this new structure are aligned with your true self and purpose.

As we commit ourselves further to this journey, cutting the cord to these old patterns and structures means confronting our denials, patterns of blame and avoidance. Eventually, as we release these childhood issues and burdens, we embrace ourselves as the mature, complex, wise and divine being that we truly are.

It is a journey, and taking the next step, however uncomfortable, gets us closer to who we truly are becoming. Go well.

Revealing and Hiding from Your Purpose

All the things you so passionately desire on your life's path, are all there to both reveal and hide your purpose. These may be money, relationships, sex, success, family and children, safety and security, knowledge and adventure.

All of these goals and desires, and there is nothing wrong with any of them, are there to help you on your journey by providing opportunities to both gain and lose them all. Achieving these goals does not mean you have achieved your soul's purpose but rather they act as a catalyst for you to fulfil your life's purpose.

Your goals uncover your desires, your creativity, and your potential. Their achievement can enhance these qualities and bring forth your growth and capacity to achieve more.

But their purpose in serving you can also be to enhance your ability to hide, avoid and cover over your fears, anxieties and wounds. By endlessly setting goals to achieve more, many people become disconnected from themselves and their inner reality. In doing so, they become pawns of their unconscious motivations and energies.

There are many world champions who have been motivated by fear, afraid of letting someone down, fulfilling someone else's expectations, or filling an empty void within themselves.

But always on your Hero's Journey, there comes a point of clarity when you just *know*. You *know* you don't have to follow that path of familiarity, of striving and desire anymore. This is a gathering point where energies and awareness come together, and you know what the simple right action is. And it's normally very ordinary.

This is where intuition and the movement of your Soul, leads you to appreciate yourself and your journey so much more than you ever could if you simply got everything that you wanted, when you wanted it. This is the purpose of the Hero's Journey. It is so much more profound than that depicted in Marvel comic movies or even in your vision boards or your affirmations. It is a Journey to fulfil your soul's purpose here on earth, and it is as easy and difficult as that.

Awareness isn't a Fixed Point

It's wonderful to know, but hard to experience the ever-changing and expanding nature of *awareness*. Many people believe and experience that awareness as a fixed point; something to defend and create an identity around. This is where the ego triumphs.

But awareness is a changing expression of the freedom of your consciousness, *and* the experience is often painful, as you move from one state of awareness to the next. You may have established a definite territory around your 'awareness', and the knowledge and practices, and sense of Self which define that state. This could be in your dietary, spiritual and political practices and beliefs.

Inevitably, someone comes along with a different experience or understanding than you. Just their presence then can trigger you into a defensive position and move to repel them, as you feel your territory threatened. This can happen in relationships, at work or in spiritual groups. It can show up by someone having a different diet, a different spiritual practice, not believing what you do, or just looking and living differently.

But this triggering is showing you precisely where the next stage of your awakening will occur. And this is just the first part of your journey. This is a journey of the Innocent, the naive, the Fool and the Knight. It is where your immature Self is beginning their journey into the experience of awareness. It is not something just to know intellectually, you must embody this new knowledge for you to gain the gifts needed to go through your journey and complete your purpose. But for something new to come into your consciousness, space needs to be created, by getting rid of the old.

In the great tale The Fisher King, Parsifal the young, naive Knight, goes through the first part of his journey blundering, rescuing and fighting. Eventually though, tired, worn-out and bruised, he finally enters the Grail Castle and asks the King the simple question that brings forth his humility and his sense of mature service for the world: "What ails thee?"

This is also illustrated in The Heroine's Journey. In the first three stages of the Journey, the Heroine (You) leaves their Known World by separating from and even rejecting the feminine. (The feminine being qualities of nature, natural cycles, being, and qualities of caring and nurturing, etc.) They then embrace the masculine energies of outwardly focussed activity, achievement and validation. They then experience success in this world and develop a territory and identity to defend.

Success in this world is achieved by denying their inherent and integral qualities of the feminine within them. This leads to an internal sense of unease that something is missing. There is a growing discomfort and awareness that their success, which they have put so much effort and focus into achieving, is actually an illusion, and can be lost.

This provides the opening for the calling of your soul. It is calling you to go on your Hero(ine)'s Journey. It is showing you that your awareness, focus and values must change. They are not a fixed point. Your awareness is there to serve you. You are not there to serve it. It is through you that the healing of the world takes place. And awareness is most often gained through suffering and humility, not just through revelation and achievement.

This journey brings forth experience, which then, with the magical gift of awareness, brings forth wisdom, healing and maturity; the very things that will heal and change the world. The things you went forth on your quest to achieve.

Questions and Exercises:

1. Give some thought as to when, where and how you 'Crossed a Threshold' in your life.
   - Name three of these occasions. Eg: your family life, your workplace, in your education.
   - What were the gifts and the pressures this Threshold moment brought to you?
   - What archetypes did this Crossing a Threshold moment bring up for you? Eg: the Hero, the Victim, the Healer, the Magical Child, the Pioneer, the Teacher etc?
2. Looking back, what three things do you think you were supposed to learn from Crossing this Threshold?
3. How did you refuse the Call to cross this Threshold?
4. What pressures were upon you to Cross the Threshold? What pressures were upon you to stay and not Cross the Threshold?
   - How did you make your decision to go or stay?
5. Name three things from this part of the book that moved you or struck you as important.
6. Creative expression - drawing: Take some time to find a quiet space. Breathe deeply and relax your body. Feel the breath go all the way through your body, and clear your mind. With paper, coloured pencils or crayons in front of you, ask yourself clearly, "Show me what is important for me to know from this part of the book."

Then, with your non-dominant hand, choose a pencil or crayon, and start drawing. It doesn't matter what it looks like, just create. Change hands when your body tells you. Repeat.

Phase 2: Initiation

Initiation sees the Hero cross a significant threshold and move into the Unknown World.

In the beginning, the Hero's Journey is about achievement. It is about having goals and dreams, and creating plans to manifest them, or fighting those who stand against them. These all represent external achievements that often launch you into your Journey

But through the course of this external quest, the Journey transitions into an emphasis on internal growth that inevitably leads to transformation.

This is primarily done through the Road of Trials. Where You (the Hero), experiences challenges, temptations, allies and enemies.

These challenges intensify, eventually leading you into an Abyss: a place of darkness, despair and symbolic or actual death.

But this too shall pass, and eventually, with the help of allies, mentors and guides, you emerge anew into the stage of Rebirth and Transformation.

Stage 3:
The Road of Trials

Along the Hero's Journey, you will encounter many trials and challenges. This is the beginning of your journey into Initiation.

Initially, you will be accompanied by friends and allies to help you achieve your goals. But you will also encounter enemies and others who will distract you, take things away from you, or prevent you from achieving your quest. This may trigger doubts and fears, illnesses, or defensive patterns to raise your anxiety and intensity.

Your ability to identify obstructions on your path, both internally and externally, and align yourself with supporting people and energies, is crucial to your growth and effective movement through this stage.

Artist: Dimitris Vetsikis

The Way of the Courageous Vulnerable

This is the way of courage (*cour* being from the heart), of maturity of being and walking your path, not just living a conceptual and righteous way.

The courageous vulnerable is the one walking through the doorway to experience the emptiness that clears the path to safety and abundance. The Alpha and the Omega.

She is the one willing to face the shadow, to look in the mirror, and finally find the gifts of love and value and power looking back at him.

He is the one willing to feel into his body, to acknowledge the places of strength and softness, of hardness and vulnerability.

She is willing to accept the movements in and through her body, of feeling and awareness, of awakening and dullness, of power and injury.

The Courageous Vulnerable acknowledges your body as the tool of your awakening, consciousness and compassion.

It's not the way of Narcissus. The one who looks outside of themselves for approval or appreciation, distraction or avoidance. This can last for a short time to provide a sense of confidence and survival. But it cannot last, it cannot abide long-term. Falling in love with your own image, by being superior to others (being more spiritual, more righteous or having the right things) and looking for an Echo (a partner or friendship group), doesn't lead to fulfilment or satisfaction, long-term.

Eventually, the authentic Self must rise, and the Courageous Vulnerable shows the way. They show the way by allowing feeling, all feeling (sadness, grief, uncertainty or fear) through to awaken their consciousness.

This can feel like things are totally out of control for a time. It can feel like the whole structure is breaking down.

That's because it is.

But like the flight of Icarus, you cannot fly away from the earth, or from your authentic self, from your feelings or from the consequences of your experiences, for extended periods, without you eventually crashing back down to earth. This *is* awakening.

This crash is the death of the childish Innocent within you. It's where you stop looking outside of yourself for love and approval, for that sense of safety, or for achievement. It may mean that you stop trying to save other people, save the world, or defend your walls and shields. It's where your illusions, delusions and denials are finally laid to rest.

This can happen through tragedy, bad luck or betrayal. But either way, you are brought to our knees.

It's where you finally take responsibility for yourself and accept who you are and where you are right now.

It means you begin again, and you are humbled.

The Courageous Vulnerable is willing to be humbled and to serve. Gone are the grandiose visions, plans and entitlements, replaced by the growing simple joy of service, surrendering, and a willingness to put one foot in front of the other.

The Courageous Vulnerable shows you the *nobility of the ordinary*, and how simply powerful this is. They show you the way into trust again. To trust yourself, to trust relationships, and to trust the world, all over again.

This is renewal. This is growth. And this is happening. Now.

You Don't Lose by Loving

Love is a verb. It is a doing word, not a thing. It is not a possession. You don't lose by loving. You can and will be hurt for sure. But you don't lose by loving.

Many people are afraid that these truisms are not actually true because they have been hurt, betrayed and abandoned. So, they shut down, close off, put up walls, barriers and shields, and defend themselves with swords, shields and armour.

But our great journey is into opening. It is into revealing ourselves as conduits for more love, not less. Our journey is not to learn how to lock ourselves away from the very experience we all want so much; to love and be loved. Our journey is to open ourselves to love. Even if it hurts. And the only way to do so is through our vulnerability.

You don't lose by loving. You can and will be hurt by doing so; that's part of the journey.

Shutting down and closing off is a normal and natural response to betrayal, hurt and abuse. You need to survive.

But you don't thrive and live in the thrall of love, by living in a protective armoured shell. And the energy needed to carry and maintain all that armour is enormous.

That you must go through times of darkness and pressure, breaking you down and pulling you apart, is part of the process of your life's journey. This is so old wounds and deeply held energies can be burnt off and dissolved. This is natural. It is part of your journey through the process of alchemy; that process of profound transformation.

The only purpose of this experience of suffering and destruction is to clear the path for the rise of a new being. It is the process whereby a new self is created to walk anew in the world.

This is the true meaning of alchemy, to transform and transmute the dark and leaden energies you carry in your human form, into the golden loving light energy being that you truly are.

We are wondrous receptors, generators and expressers of love and care, and it is your journey to become the greatest receptor and expressor of love and light that you came here to be.

You don't lose by loving. You can and will be hurt for sure. But you don't lose by loving. You become the vessel of blessing. And this is a great thing, it is the path of a truly inspirational, creative and purposeful life.

Who Are You When You Don't Get What You Want?

In the Hero's Journey, not getting what you want is often when the Shadow comes out and takes over. This is when the archetypes of the Bully, Manipulator, Blamer, Avoider, Attacker, Destroyer, Victim, or Wounded Child, take over and rule.

Or perhaps the Shadow turns inward, and you become the Recluse, to nurture feelings of abandonment and woundedness, and become isolated, bitter and cynical.

Sometimes these expressions of anger and righteousness are given noble or spiritual names, justifications, and rationalisations, like calling yourself a Goddess or a Warrior.

But all these energies are like waves created in a tempest on the ocean. Eventually, they do subside. Their fury is abated. Their energy may have been directed and expended upon some structure, or even another human being. This brings a short-term feeling of power and righteousness but doesn't actually resolve the problem. Venting our disappointment and fury upon another human being doesn't satisfy the emptiness of our woundedness.

When you have awareness over what is moving through you, you can seek outside counsel or a healer to assist you in moving this energy through you, safely.

When you do so, eventually the energy of fury and woundedness is abated and healed. It is then returned to the power of the source, or the wider universe, which absorbs all of it back into its powerful embrace.

Nature is a great healer, perhaps the greatest. Who then is better able to absorb and transmute your disappointment at not getting what you want? Nature, the earth and all its power and capacity? Or a human being? With all their insecurities, fears and doubts and unresolved wounds?

We have enormous expectations of others and what they 'should' do for us, and what they 'should' do for the world. But sometimes life and nature bring you the greatest healing mechanisms, literally, right under your feet. The answers are not 'out there', but within us.

Maybe spend some time listening to nature; feel the earth beneath your feet, swim in the ocean, feel the strength in a tree, and feel the acceptance there is for you. Remember to love always. It is always there for you.

The Gift of Stress and Discomfort

As the great storyteller, Rabbi Dr. Abraham Twerski (yes, that is his real name), tells us in his wonderful lobster metaphor, stress and discomfort are the signs in the body that it is time to grow. And you must attend to it, otherwise, it will become very, *very* uncomfortable for you and those around you.

Rabbi Twerski tells us that a lobster is a soft-bodied animal that lives inside a rigid shell. As the lobster grows, it finds the shell very confining. It finds itself under-pressure and uncomfortable in an undersized shell. When this happens, it goes under a rock formation to protect itself. It casts off its old shell, then spends some time letting the new shell form and harden around its newly exposed and expanded, soft body. Once this occurs, it can then go back out into the ocean and continue its life as a bigger lobster in a bigger shell.

Eventually though, as this new shell also becomes too rigid and too small, the lobster feels the discomfort, and must repeat the process of expelling the old shell, to continue growing.

He emphasises that the stimulus for the lobster to grow is its discomfort. For humans too, the signs for us to grow is when we feel uncomfortable and stressed. Rabbi Twerski shows us that it is important to acknowledge and value these times of pressure and adversity as essential for our growth and expansion.

By attending to these signs of pressure and adversity, as uncomfortable as they may be, we can bring more love and care to ourselves. By consciously spending the time to go to the depths needed to break free from our old shell, we ensure that we embody new patterns of awareness in our lives. We can then become bigger, happier lobsters within our bigger shells, ready to engage more fully with the world.

Going through Hard Times

Going through hard times is the experience of enduring great emotional, spiritual and physical change. It's not easy, but it is essential. It is essential that we discover that *we* are the ones who will rescue and comfort ourselves, it is not 'out there'.

To demonstrate, a friend recently wrote, "No, heartbreak is not easy. As one of the fierce and wrathful emanations of love, it will throw you off at times. It will pull the rug out from under you and remind you of how fragile

*"Truth is like poetry.
And most people fucking hate poetry."*

**From the movie,
The Big Short**

it really is to be here. But no matter how difficult or confusing things may be, you can start right now.

Slow way down. Breathe deeply. Attune to the heartbroken one inside you and start a new world.

As you make experiential, embodied, and intimate contact with the tender one within, you can finally meet her. You can hold him. And you can renew your vow to never, ever abandon who you are.

Keep this one close, feel the unseen ones all around you, and give your heart to this world."

The Victim Gets a Bad Rap

You shouldn't be a Victim. You're not supposed to be a Victim. It's not right to be a Victim. You are not allowed to be a Victim. If you are a Victim, you deserve it.

Yet... we all go through this stage of life. It seems then that it is a natural stage in our journey into growth and maturity. Yet we are not allowed to acknowledge or accept our Victimhood. We are told we must fight it and resist this stage of our life, as it is the lowest vibration a human can emanate, or so they say. You, therefore, are not allowed to acknowledge, nor accept what is happening to you. So, what do you do now?

As previously mentioned, author Caroline Myss speaks of four universal survival-oriented archetypes: the Child, the Prostitute, the Saboteur and the Victim. These four archetypes play vital roles in helping us create our identity and values and help us fulfil our soul contracts. It is important to note that we experience these archetypes both in their *light* or noble aspect, *and* also in their *shadow*.

The *shadow* is that part of yourself you deny, don't acknowledge or are not aware of. At first, this side of yourself is unconscious. It could show up as doubt, envy or jealousy, sabotage or judgement towards others. But as you gain self-awareness, you begin to acknowledge your *shadow* tendencies rather than denying them, shunning them, or blaming someone else for them. This is the first stage of healing and making yourself *whole*.

The Child archetype embodies innocence and purity, wonder and awe. However, as you grow, you will experience betrayal, lack of safety, untruthfulness, and importantly, abandonment in your life. This leads to your wounding, and the shadow comes forth to help you survive by providing boundaries or armour to shield you from your circumstances. When in your shadow, you may become petulant, demanding, needy, or untrusting, aggressive and defensive towards others. Your focus is outside of you, as this is where the perceived threat comes from. The shadow may also come forth as a defence system such as denial. Denial is the most powerful way to suppress your woundedness, disappointment and pain, and it enables you to survive.

The Prostitute archetype is about value and worth. It shows up when you are asked to compromise your values and integrity to survive or succeed. The Prostitute is active often in your relationships and in your work, as you feel pressured to make decisions out of fear, obligation or lack. You are often put into compromises and dilemmas where you must choose between circumstances that may benefit others and their agenda, and those that don't necessarily benefit you at all.

The Saboteur is about self-worth and safety. It comes up to undermine or betray you and others to retain your position in the familiar, known and therefore 'safe' world. This is the familiar pattern of the Victim. It is important to note that the Child within us perceives familiarity as safe, paradoxically, even if this environment is toxic and abusive.

The Victim archetype is about power and powerlessness. There are many times in your life, especially when you are a child, where you will naturally experience dependence and have little or no power over your circumstances.

As an adult, you will still experience the Victim, not because you have done anything wrong or bad, but because the archetype is still active in your life. It does so to ensure you wake up into the next greater, and more mature stage in your journey. The Victim presents in the form of powerlessness, dependency, or neediness. Its purpose is to get you to finally say "No" to your habitual and familiar responses, and eventually say "Yes" (however meekly) to your soul's path. And this path can only be walked in humility.

Like many people, I have experienced long periods of powerlessness, having: no money, no job, no career, no energy, no health, no relationships, no car, no power and no effectiveness in the world. I felt humiliated, and seemingly completely worthless and powerless. The Victim was clearly an important and active archetype in my life. I had power over nothing, and I felt utterly ashamed of myself and my role in my circumstances.

And yet... I would always get up. I always sensed that there was some greater purpose to my life and that there was some highly valuable element within me, which only I knew and could see, and it was my job to persevere long enough for it to emerge.

Failure and powerlessness are not only extremely uncomfortable to experience, but also to witness. Western culture is very achievement and success-oriented, as indicated by The Heroine's Journey, and so accepting Victimhood as a natural part of your development and growth makes it even more uncomfortable to acknowledge. You *must,* however, experience these times of powerlessness so you can be led into humility, and the one choice that leads inevitably to your freedom.

However, to get to that place of choice you must face your fears and denials, which are the greatest of all your survival strategies. Denial is there to keep you safe from the false beliefs and wounds that you believe will ultimately lead to your destruction. But this belief is false and must be exposed as such. Hence, you go through a 'Road of Trials', to eventually get you to that place where you must face the truth of who you are.

Facing the darkness, the demons and dragons that have grown within you as a result of suppressing or bypassing your feelings and woundedness is truly your great calling and one of your life's primary purposes. Uncovering these untrue beliefs, hidden in the maze of your psyche, is a courageous journey into your vulnerability.

Emerging from this experience brings forth a great sense of liberation and achievement. You may have released yourself from an inherited journey; that of living through your ancestral and familial issues of abuse, addiction, or poverty.

The New Age and human potential movements, however, with all their affirmations and goal setting, vision boards and grandiose 'I Am...'

statements, may actually keep you in the Victim archetype longer than necessary. This is because they don't acknowledge or allow for the *gift* of the Victim to show itself. By not acknowledging and respecting your Victim, you feed your denial and resistance of what is happening in your body, your behaviour, and psyche.

But even this path of creating survival strategies like denial and blame, and their eventual breakdown, is a natural part of your journey. Denying these aspects keeps you in the illusion and delusion of control.

But truly, these patterns cannot last. They are not supposed to. And the more you create a vessel of support around you, through therapy or groups, or friendship networks, the more you can honestly look at yourself and embrace your fears, wounds, and darkness.

By completing this journey, you become free to move to the next stage of your life. That is to fulfil your next great life purpose and mission: the freedom to express your heart and soul fully and truly in this world. This is what builds trust, love, and faith, and creates the New World you wrote down in your affirmations and visualised in your Vision Boards all those months and years before.

It's Hard Living a Pure Life

Recently, I watched a David Attenborough program on African elephants. The elephants would go to a certain spot in their territory and eat dirt. They would dig into the cliffs there and spray the mineral-rich dirt into their mouths and onto their bodies. The whole herd would wallow in the dirt and mud, and the young ones enjoyed playing in the spray and the muck.

They were doing this, eating dirt because they couldn't get the minerals and nutrients they needed from their common diet of grasses and leaves. So, the elephants would go off on an excursion every so often to gorge themselves in caves and other mineral-rich sites, to find the nutrition they needed to sustain themselves.

Humans do similar things; we just judge ourselves and others very harshly when we go on these excursions. These actions become part of a Shadow life and a Shadow world which is mostly denied and shamed. But what if these men, women, and children are going on these excursions into their Shadow worlds to find the 'nutrition' or the energetic expression they need to fill the emptiness they feel inside? What if the diet and lifestyle they live in their Known World cannot sustain the needs of their complex psyches and soul contracts? What if these excursions were part of a healing journey? A journey to heal undigested trauma and deeply held wounds? How do you judge them then?

Most people, however, go through stages of trying to do the right thing and live good lives. They get jobs, start relationships, and live a lifestyle that reflects their common understanding. This is what is expected.

But for many, there comes a time when they feel something is missing. Something is not right. They are not receiving the essential minerals and nutrients they need for their soul life in their Known World. They then turn to a Shadow life. This life houses their anguish, heartache and deeply held wounds. It is a life which communicates with unconsciously held hurts and wounds from past lives or inter-generational issues. So, what do they need to do? How do they get the nutrition and quality of energy they need to fulfil these Shadow or Soul needs?

This is where you will look outside of yourself and go on an excursion 'out there' to find the missing *nutrients* you need. The problem is, you don't know what they are, and so you may go on seemingly destructive forays into the Shadow world. This even occurs with those living the most *right* and *intentional* lives. They may be religious people, or yoga and meditation practitioners, or those who read all the spiritual texts. Yet still, they feel something is missing. Something is living in the Shadow which is calling to be acknowledged and fed within them.

The answers lie in being open and honest about what is happening within you. Seeking outside counsel helps in keeping you safe through this journey. This is best done by a professional, or someone who can provide confidential discussions. Beware of openly sharing these Shadow elements of fears, doubts and uncertainties within a family or a relationship, as it may prove very problematic. These well-meaning people may not have the maturity, awareness, or capability to listen and provide the understanding you need.

However, to not acknowledge these movements within you often leads to self-destructive tendencies, or into more extreme external expressions of these Shadow needs.

But always, when you are going through times of change and uncertainty, there needs to be an expression of love and kindness towards yourself and others. This is how you heal. It is through nurturing and care, not through judgement.

Uncomfortable Feelings

Times of discomfort are there to lead you into growth. These times begin with an awareness that something deeper and bigger is calling you. You

then have a choice: acknowledge and engage with what is happening, or ignore it, avoid it, or blame someone or something around you.

Deep-level wounding doesn't get resolved by ignoring it or avoiding it. It gets transmuted by acknowledging the feeling, experiencing it and allowing it to flow. This is where many New Age, 'positive-thinking' and self-development movements have not served us well. Concepts such as 'change your thoughts and you change your outcomes' alone don't deal with the reality of the depth and complexity of the trauma, energies and experiences we go through.

Suppressing the feeling through activity (working, sexing, meditating, drugging, drinking or exercising) is a common way to deny and avoid the discomfort. Medications (including alcohol and drugs) are also commonly used and socially acceptable ways of avoiding the feelings and wounds, which are trying to be heard.

But the soul knows. The soul knows how to help you heal. The soul will put you in contact with people or things that will move through your armour and defences, and trigger or touch that wounded part of you. These are the times of breakthrough. They may also look like times of breakdown.

The breakthrough could look like an eruption, a lashing out at others, with emotional rants filled with blame and bitterness. That part of you that has kept you safe for so long, your ego and defences, are being put under pressure to change and adapt. They are being shown that they have limitations and weaknesses. That's why through the build-up of pressure, these pent-up energies must vent themselves. These limitations can include the failure of your grandiose plans and ideas, the failure of others to live up to unrealistic expectations, or your fantasies of control over your environment through your thoughts, behaviours and rituals of 'manifestation' and 'co-creation'.

The pressure and stress of your adversity are there precisely to make you take the action you have so desperately been avoiding; to release the old shell and identity (your old comfort-zone), and walk into a new identity, creating uncertainty about present and future outcomes, but also bringing a sense of freshness and aliveness as you move further into your vulnerability.

Throughout my life, I have often felt deep discomfort and uncertainty within myself, especially during the early 2000s, when I was ill for long periods. I felt depressed over my inability to change what was happening in my body or my circumstances. During these times I experienced deep shame, guilt, depression and a strong sense of powerlessness.

Ten years or so later, when my health was stronger, I experienced periods of intense anger and frustration rising within me. I knew then that I had a choice as to how to deal with these experiences; engage with these uncomfortable feelings, try to ignore them, or be 'positive' and 'forgive' them so they would go away. I knew the latter two methods never worked for me, having tried many times over the years. So, however reluctantly, I would always engage these feelings, and I went through a disciplined process to do so.

Engaging a Healing Process

I have experienced deep discomfort in the build-up of emotions and energies in my body over many years. These build-ups would often last several days. But eventually, I found a way to deal with these feelings and energies.

I would get up out of bed, or sit mindfully in a chair, and deliberately and completely acknowledge and engage with what was happening within me at that moment. I would go through a process of welcoming the feelings into my awareness and into my body. I would always begin with breathing deeply, feeling the breath all the way through my body. I would stand or sit openly, mindfully, and in a balanced and aware way. This was my way of setting my intention for healing through engagement.

I would then begin the process by breathing slowly and with intention. My stomach would push out, naturally drawing in a breath and bringing my awareness into the lower parts of my body. I am thereby intentionally creating space in my body for something new to come in. This breathing technique anchors me into the process, and signals to my soul and higher Self, that I am ready and serious about engaging with what happens next.

I then allow the feeling to come into my awareness and into my body. I experience the feeling and intensity fully. My body often convulses or constricts severely during these times. But quickly, like the flow of a wave crashing and dissipating onto the shore, the energy would rise to its climax, and then slowly flow away out of my body and out of my field. My body would then quickly relax and feel more open and clear.

Afterwards, I might write about my awareness, or draw a picture symbolising the new flow of energy within me. This whole process might take anywhere between fifty seconds to three minutes. After a brief rest, if I felt there was still more energy to be engaged with, I would repeat the process again.

By engaging these feelings and energies, I acknowledge that my soul, through my body, is leading me. My soul is leading me to my vulnerability, which then leads me to clear anything that is not aligned with my most authentic and powerful Self.

To do so, I must clear any and all dark energies and false beliefs I carry in my system and my auric field. I cannot remain as the old self, with all its fantasy-based grandiose visions, or as the depressed and isolated Self. I know that I must lose everything, to have it all. I **must** lose *everything*, to have it all.

Your soul wants you to wake up and free yourself of the falsehoods and restrictions that have ruled you or controlled you throughout your life. And releasing these familiar patterns of thought and energy can be deeply uncomfortable work. However, it is necessary for you to fulfil your soul contracts.

It means you cannot carry those old hurts and wounds from childhood, from your marriage or past relationships, or from unfair work experiences with you anymore. You cannot carry these unconscious memories from past lives either. You must find the way through to release them from your field and reintegrate any lost or shunned parts of yourself. By doing so, you lead yourself, inexorably, into freedom.

This is your responsibility and your soul's purpose in this lifetime. To do so is definitely a Hero's Journey.

What to Do on Your Journey

On my journey, there were long periods when I didn't do anything sexy or exciting or achieve any grand goal. I just basically followed my intuition and the intelligence inherent in my body. I let my body lead me.

This meant I learnt how to relax when I was sick. I learnt how to move and take action when I was called to. It meant that at times I was isolated and didn't have any interaction with the world. This was all part of my journey into Initiation. And afterwards came the experience of integrating these diverse energies.

I didn't attend rallies or get involved with causes. I didn't go to ecstatic dances or meditation circles. I unsubscribed from a bunch of newsletters and groups, and just got down to the solid and ordinary work of experiencing new energies, new vibrations and new understandings, and then integrating them into my body and being. This meant spending a *lot* of time alone and resting.

The energies of full and new moons, the eclipses, and the other planetary and solar shifts we have had over the last few years, affected me profoundly. My energy was often incredibly low, and I felt extremely slow and fatigued in my body. I would often wake up with the 'fuzzies', a dullness throughout my body, which would last for many hours. I sometimes got confused, often having a hard time concentrating or remembering, and this would take most of the day to integrate and get back to 'normal'. But always I knew that everything was alright and that I was doing exactly what I was supposed to, even though it was uncomfortable and seemed like I was achieving nothing at the time.

I knew I was on a journey of building profound trust. That is trust within myself; trust that there really is a big picture and big process of change and transformation going on, and this is moving through me and others around the world.

I also had to trust my ability to discern; to listen and be guided by my intuition, my senses, and by the universe. I know I am involved in a great time of completion and renewal, and I know I am fulfilling my part, even if it is deeply wearisome and difficult at times.

I have also witnessed many others go through this same cycle of completion, transformation, and integration. These people were often in various states and levels of awareness, acceptance, or denial and resistance; blaming themselves or others for the state of the world or the state they were in.

I learnt that you don't transform without challenges. The challenge is there for you to evoke your highest self, to take responsibility, to make decisions accordingly and then act. This is hard. The challenge brings up old wounds, old practises, old paradigms that directly affect your ego, your identity and your sense of certainty and control. These dilemmas are essential in aligning you with your true values and purpose. They help you determine what is a '*Yes*' and what is a '*No*'. Just having this simple awareness builds confidence and trust.

I witnessed many who went through this pathway in the process of inevitable change. Many of whom embodied huge resistance to their circumstances and suffered accordingly. Often, they went into periods of great intensity of focussing on causes, old dreams and goals and ways to save the world. They seemed to be pushing themselves so far that something had to break.

Several people I know pushed themselves to the utmost extremes that placed them in the path of death. This was a *bifurcation* point. That is, a point where the old structure cannot process any more information, and only a completely new structure can handle the new thinking, perception, and vibration they will hold. Eventually, after intense medical care, these people did emerge with a new appreciation of themselves and the world. They finally realised; they didn't have to do it *all on their own* anymore.

For me, I practised over years, acknowledging and welcoming into my body the feelings and emotions which I knew were in my field, even if they were deeply uncomfortable or even disturbing. In this way, I was able to process and release energies ranging from the light to the dark, hateful and fear-laden energies and emotions which I carried unconsciously in my body and my field.

I didn't have to understand them or know where they came from, I just had to acknowledge them, feel them, allow them to move through me. And like a wave, they would just roll out and leave. Most often this process would take somewhere between 20-50 seconds.

So, during these times of transition, some wonderful people came into my life. They enabled me to work through issues and be mentors or guides in my work life, in friendships, family or virtually through Facebook. For that, I am grateful to those who provided me with the opportunity to demonstrate my highest qualities.

I was also deeply challenged, and often joyfully so. I know I completed many old soul contracts fully and completely. It wasn't an exciting or amazing time; it was just very fulfilling and filled with purpose.

How Emptiness Works in Relationships

How does emptiness work in relationships and why is it useful?

In relationships, emptiness means having the capacity to *not know*; to not know what to do or how to be, and to have that be okay. It means being able to hold someone without knowing the answer to their problems. It means listening and allowing them to go through their state-of-being at that time, without being attached to the content of what is being said or expressed. This is hard to do, especially if you are being attacked in the process.

Emptiness means releasing and clearing your field of wounds and energy patterns that don't serve you anymore. Emptying is also commonly referred to as purging. After the purge, there is space now for allowing an *ease of flow*. It does not mean passiveness, disconnection or disengagement.

It means listening. Listening for feeling; listening for the feeling the other person is expressing. When you hear the feeling and can name it, that is the most courageous, and oftentimes, most confronting part of a conversation. This is empathy in action.

Being empty doesn't mean you have nothing to do, or that you feel nothing, it means you can hold a space of safety. It means allowing the other to speak and be, without the need to assert or defend your beliefs, sense of self and knowing. This then becomes an ego battle.

You show profound courage and strength of character to hold yourself steady amidst the turmoil that happens in your daily life. It is especially difficult when someone close to you is in a state of high emotion and is expressing all of that, directly *at* you. To stand in that maelstrom of energy and emotion, and hold yourself still, with your boundaries strong and not attached to the words or content, is truly an act of courage. It is an act of trust and respect and strength.

In this situation, the other party is providing the opportunity for you to deal with what happens 'in the next moment'. This is the hard, messy and very ordinary work of being in a relationship. It is dealing with uncertainty, fear, disappointment, let-downs and the clash of styles and priorities. And this is the profound nature of what relationships provide us. They provide the opportunity to express yourself in multitudinous ways, to grow and to heal, through a deep-level connection with another human being.

Detachment is often confused with 'disengagement' and 'disconnection'. These are acts of separation and a denial of your humanity. 'Detaching' yourself however, means not identifying with the drama, the emotions and the energy that is being experienced around you. An important distinction.

Some spiritual people and practices do *not* emphasise connection; they interpret this as an attachment, which they see as 'less than' or 'wrong'. But connection and relationship *are* what we are here for. And being in the messiness of life is being *in* your life, which provides the opportunity to fulfil your Soul's purpose and mission.

I have seen many in the spiritual community aspire to disconnection and actively disengaged from the world and people and use their practice to create stronger and better shields and armour. They strengthen their spiritual egos and separate themselves from others. But this is not the Hero's Journey and why you are here.

You are here to engage with the world through relationships and experience a whole range of sensations and feelings. This is often uncomfortable and confusing. And opening yourself to emptiness through your vulnerability is truly courageous, and it is living to your potential, in the noblest and most ordinary of ways.

The Purpose of Emotional Pain

Pain is a normal part of life. You feel pain emotionally, mentally, physically and psychically. For some, it is an extraordinary occurrence, but for others, it is a normal part of their life and routine.

How you deal with pain is a question for the ages. There are whole industries, both legal and illegal, surrounding the mitigation, avoidance and the elimination of pain.

So, what is the pain for? What purpose does it serve, and what is the best way to deal with it?

Emotional pain is something that must happen in your life. It is part of your journey to experience disappointment, heartache and the shattering of expectations. Conflict and stress are also essential elements of a Hero's Journey. This is where your inner Child or Innocent archetype experiences the harshness of reality in this world. These experiences provide the impetus to go on your journey and discover your gifts and talents and apply them in the world.

As an adult though, you must adopt a relationship with pain that enables you to live effectively. You must then find ways to consciously connect with it, and thereby honour its place in your life.

The challenge of emotional pain is not only to acknowledge the feelings that are there, but also to acknowledge the personal nature of them. This includes acknowledging the experiences and circumstances that brought them into your field. In doing so, you cry out in pain, "Why? Why did she/he/they do this to me? How could these 'loving' caregivers do that to me?" In doing so, you experience the intense feelings of abandonment, disappointment and heartbreak.

The process of healing occurs first by acknowledging the energy of the pain and allowing it to be. Only then can you direct loving energy within. This allows the energy to move on, and out of your field. This process provides the resolution of a soul contract. It is the courageous movement from being a Wounded Child-adult, into a healed, self-loving, self-appreciating mature adult.

Through your awareness, you can direct the love and care you are seeking to your own heart and your innocence. You then become the *lover* you are searching for. You are the *one* who will say the words you so want and need to hear.

You then become the alchemist's vessel, transmuting those uncomfortable, low and dark energies, into vibrations of golden light and matter. This benefits all and provides a pathway to your greater freedom, and to the freedom of the collective.

Sometimes life just sucks. It just does, and you need to be the best friend and lover you can be to yourself.

This is your soul's work, and this is your soul's purpose until it is done. I am so grateful to those who do this simple and courageous work of healing and making themselves whole. They are the ones who are the true world changers.

Limitations of Your Own Power

"Just do your work. And if the world needs your work it will come and get you. And if it doesn't, do your work anyway. You can have fantasies about having control over the world, but I know I can barely control my kitchen sink. That is the grace I'm given. Because when one can control things, one is limited to one's own vision."

Kiki Smith – Artist

Oftentimes it's hard to acknowledge the limitations of your power. The Warrior and personal achievement cultures of recent years have defined happiness as being getting what you want, when you want it (Now!). This means you should always: be in control, have love, be in love, be appreciated and acknowledged, be super fit and healthy, always succeed, have lots of money, and always be *right*!

But life just ain't that way. Life is *not* fair. We *do* get sick, we *do* experience heartache and unfairness and betrayal. It's not because you attracted it to you with your thoughts as is commonly repeated. We *do* get betrayed by loved ones and significant people in our lives, and experience hardship and loss.

They say, energy goes where attention flows. As you embody more of your wisdom and compassion, you stop concentrating on what everybody else is doing 'out there'.

You stop trying to change everybody else to make them believe what you believe, and you realise that changing and loving your Self, is truly the most conscious and most loving thing we can do. This is you work. This is the work that truly changes the world.

So, by putting your attention and energy where it is most effective in achieving change, healing and satisfaction for yourself (your work), you bring love and relief to the collective, whether anyone else knows it or not.

But as Kiki Smith says above, "Just do your work". Your work will *always* be about experiencing the transformation that is brought through your journey. It's *not* about the trophies and the finish lines, although these are very nice, and are also part of your journey. It really is all about the *transformation*, the healing, and the learning. And in doing your *work*, you fulfil your soul's purpose. And this is where the freedom and ultimate satisfaction and fulfilment come from. It is in doing your work.

"He that is without sin among you, let him first cast a stone at her." John 8:7

I think there would be vast lines of people queueing up to throw stones today.

I thought about this quote during the 2016 US elections. There is so much righteousness being thrown around by people who 'know everything' and 'get everything right', (the *right* way to see and experience the world, the *right* companies to protest against, etc) that there seem to be legions of people without sin who are throwing stones.

I found myself imagining the following Monty Python-esque scene, inspired by their 1979 film 'The Life of Brian'. Imagine Eric Idle as a stall owner selling rocks in a dusty market, with Terry Gilliam in the stall next to him.

Eric Idle: Get yer rocks here. Stoning s'afternoon. Get yer igneous, metamorphic, and sedimentary rocks here. All Vegan-approved. Dairy free. Not tested on animals. Made only for stoning humans.

STAGE 3: THE ROAD OF TRIALS

<Terry Jones, dressed as a woman, steps up to the stall>

Eric Idle: Ullo madam, what can I do for you?

Terry Jones: I want something to last. Not yer cheap conglomerate rubbish. Breaks up after only five throws. Although last time, I threw it at a Samaritan, it broke up, he came back with all the pieces and apologised. Nice chap. Centurion stuck him with a sword, said he was littering. Anyway, I want something with a bit of quality.

Eric Idle: Say no more madam! How about some granite?! It's got weight and will last a lifetime. Guaranteed not to scratch for the first one hundred throws.

Oh, and if you want class and quality, you can't go past marble! How about this? If Jehovah was throwing stones, He'd choose marble. Oh, (leans closer and in a loud whisper) and it is said that an Eye-talian fellow called Michael Angelo is doing some sculptures with it too. Newds…if ya know what I mean (and taps his nose with a wink)….say no more…

Terry Jones: Yes, yes alright. I'll have five granites, half a dozen marble, some slate, and some pumice for my daughter.

Eric Idle: Pumice…good choice madam; spewed out from a volcano, made in a fire, yet light, and easy to carry. Just right for a virtuous young woman.

<Terry Jones leaves>

<John Cleese approaches>

John Cleese: Hello yes, I was wanting some stones for righteous indignation, spiritual awakening and denial.

Eric Idle: Well step right this way sir! Spirituality sir, we've got a full range. Crystals sir… look at these beauties. It is said sir, that when you hit someone with a crystal, it opens up their chakras. It's an act of awakening, sir. You, sir, are then a vehicle for enlightenment. It's really a community service with one throw.

We've also got river stones, some from the holy river Ganges, which have carvings from elite shamans which say, 'Namaste' on them. Which means when it hits them, it gives 'em a blessing. You should be commended, sir.

Oh, and here we have stones with sacred geometric patterns on them, which means when you hit the villain, it sends them into another dimension. Amazing.

Oh, and just in sir... Law of Attraction stones... said to be blessed by Abraham himself. You throw it at them, and it says, 'You are attracting this to you'. Good also for denial and righteous indignation. Very popular these days.

John Cleese: Yes, yes. I'll have two of each. Oh, do you have any yoga stones? I do yoga you see.

Eric Idle: Yoga stones. Absolutely, sir. Right this way, sir. Before you, sir, are stones from Rishikesh in India, prayed over by gurus and ascetic masters over hundreds of years. Good for motivation, spirituality and of course, righteous indignation too sir. They are inscribed with mantras like: 'Move yer Asana!', 'Stick this up yer Asana', and 'Yes, yer Asana does look big in that!'. Can't go past that sir. Good for awakening too sir, especially if you say that to yer wife.

John Cleese: Yes, yes, they all sound quite appropriate. And denial. Something for denial.

Eric Idle: Say no more! How about this one, standard issue in full caps, 'I'M NOT ANGRY!'. Or comes in lower case if you're going passive-aggressive. We've also got, "This hurts me more than it does you", "I'm not judging you!" and the timeless, "Truth hurts doesn't it".

John Cleese: Yes wonderful, I'll have three of each, and some gravel for the youngsters.

Eric Idle: Quite right, sir. Teach 'em early. *<He says with a grin and a wink>*

<John Cleese walks away>

Eric Idle: (Waving) Thank you, sir. We're open every day except Saturday. Upgrades and gift vouchers welcome. <*Turns to Terry Gilliam in the next stall as Cleese walks away*> Stupid git.

<*Continues talking to Gilliam*>

Now, as I was saying, Roman numerals are a stocktaking nightmare. You try writing 4988 pieces of gravel in Roman numerals.

Now, if they moved to Arabic numbers, well, there's boundless opportunities there...Now I told you about my mate Machmud. Well, he's got an uncle who knows this fella, who's gotta mate...

My Plans for my Life, and the Universe's Plan for Me

One of the things I discovered, however painfully, throughout my journey, is that there really is a *big* picture going on in my life.

Part of that picture is that the Universe really does have a plan for me. The painful part is that *my* plan for my life has often been very different from the Universe's plan for me.

For me, learning to listen, pay attention to, and then follow the Universe's plan has been one of the hardest things I have ever had to do. It meant letting go of my desires, my goals, my dreams, my sense of justice, my righteousness and entitlement, and surrender myself to the reality that I live in. Now.

Often this realisation came from a crisis: a crisis in health, wealth, family, relationship, or some personal injustice. It meant that I could not do it all on my own anymore. I could not do it the way I wanted to anymore. I could not change the world to the way I wanted it to be. That was not part of my life's plan. Life just didn't work like that for me. There was a bigger plan at play.

This realisation, brought on a crisis of identity, "Who am I if I am not these things that I have dedicated myself to for *all* these years?"

In my case, I got very sick. I had viruses upon viruses which totally sapped my strength and my energy. Because of this, working and earning

Love Your Self No Matter What

Enlightenment...is a process of breaking down and reconciliation.
It can be achieved through disciplined spiritual practice. But not always.
It can be achieved through chanting and hours of meditation.
But not always.
It can be achieved through worship and prayer and ceremony.
But not always.
It can be achieved through heartbreak, break-down or break-up.
It can be achieved through despair and darkness.
Enlightenment can be achieved through suffering.
But it can also be achieved through Grace.
It can be achieved through acceptance, compassion,
love and openness.
However you get there, do it! Do your work.
Have the courage
To love your Self no matter what.
This is true enlightenment.

money became very problematic and impossible at times. Eventually, I had to surrender. I had nothing left. I had to give up everything.

I decided to listen and attend to what was in front of me. Rather than judging my circumstances as 'wrong' and me 'less than' because I couldn't' support myself, I decided to engage with the world as it was at that time. I engaged with my body, my health and my resistance to what was happening.

Slowly, ever so slowly, I got some work and reluctantly engaged with the world in ways I didn't want to, but that I needed to. Eventually, I learnt to appreciate myself and those around me in these environments. I learnt that I was okay even though I was working in environments I didn't want to be in and wasn't utilising my skills to their potential.

This appreciation and gratitude became my source of freedom.

What I learnt was that the greatness of the Universe is always speaking to me. It is often through the mouths of others, and often in words and circumstances, I neither want to see nor hear.

The Universe is often saying, "Over there. Over there", or "Not here. Not Now". But because this doesn't conform to the 'right' way I had conceived of and desired, I dismissed these messages, and therefore missed the opportunity right in front of me.

I took jobs where I could find them, in sales or telemarketing. Areas that I previously thought were a sign that I was 'selling out' and compromising my values. But in taking these jobs, I met a vast array of people from a huge variety of backgrounds that I wouldn't otherwise have had the chance to. In meeting these people and talking with them, I found that most people live courageous and noble lives in very ordinary ways. Eventually, I learnt to acknowledge and see this courage and nobility even within myself.

By practising this discipline of self-love and self-appreciation, I created, quite unexpectedly, the subtle foundation of acceptance and appreciation of others in the world around me.

I know now, my journey has served me to get me to where I am; to the place where I am open and accepting of my greatest soul's purpose - that of moving into freedom, power and abundance. I also know I didn't do anything wrong to not achieve these things previously. This was all part of a grand purpose at play. A purpose of completion and fulfilment.

It is hard to release all the stuff that you think you know. It is a profound thing to let go of all the righteousness you hold, the entitlement that you believe is your due, and the judgements you have towards others, and most pointedly, the judgements you have towards yourself. But the Universe is letting you know that this stage of your life is ending, and a new, more profound life of activity and fulfilment awaits you.

So, take a few minutes today, tomorrow and the next day to say, "Thank you" to yourself for all the things you have done, achieved and survived. This is the embodiment of what more kindness, compassion and appreciation look like.

The Distinction Between 'What You Want', And 'What You Need'

What you want is to be loved. You want to be heard, appreciated, valued, acknowledged... and mostly, you want it from someone 'out there'. You want to have your lover adore you.

You want to be *in* love, and this love fills your heart and your beingness, heals your wounds, and makes you feel whole. And when you have this, you have that glorious feeling of euphoria that you want to share with others. This feeling gives you a sense of buoyancy and goodwill towards others, which brings such a sense of exhilaration, that you believe it will awaken and heal the whole world.

This is the manifestation of the Lover archetype. But it can be an expression of the *immature* Lover archetype, as its attention is mostly focussed outside of you, in a magical and romantic experience of reality.

The Lover is an energising and creative force in your life. It brings forth a sense of aliveness, vividness, and passion. It brings you into your sensory experience and awakens your desires to have more of these heightened sensations and experiences. Hence, you are moved to develop visions and goals, and lists of wants that reflect your desires.

But life and your soul's purpose aren't just about satisfying your wants and desires. Life works in cycles. Nature is impersonal. Both destruction and creation go on within a normal cycle of nature. It is naturally so.

Put Yourself First

Put your health and welfare above all else. Put it ahead of your ideas and ideals. These are from your head and won't feed your heart or soul. They lead to dissatisfaction and disappointment.

Put your health and welfare ahead of your causes and fights. Put it ahead of your projects and protests. There will always be a myriad of causes to fight. There will always be enemies to defeat, children to cry for, arguments to win, and exercises to run. Put your health and welfare ahead of your ideas and ideals.

There will always be another opportunity to make money or be employed. But there is only one You. So, take the time today to give thanks to You. You survived. You overcame. You endured. And you were gracious.

You are appreciative. You are thankful. You are thankful, even to the last person you think deserves your gratitude the most, your Self. So, take a moment and put your Self first.

The love that you seek is not 'out there'. It is in the eyes and the heart of the one you see in the mirror.

The words you wish to hear and need to hear, will not come from *him* or *her* 'out there'. They can only come from you, saying them to your Self, First. This is the love of your life.

So, put your Self first and change the world, by loving yourself, first. Say the words that you need to hear:

I see you. I appreciate you. I thank you. I love you. All ways.

And repeat.

Life is often unfair, and to achieve your life's purpose, it doesn't just give you what you want, you also need to attend to what you *need*. This is the process of maturing through your journey. And maturing is the expression and application of natural laws and cycles. It is not the same as ageing.

What you *need* is to bring your attention, your listening, your acknowledgement and your appreciation to yourself, first.

You must attend to your needs to bring you a sense of ease and fulfilment. This means attending to the reality of your fears and wounds, and bringing your healing attention to your Self. This is uncovering and remembering your true Self. This is the loving presence that you bring to yourself and is the embodiment of the Lover archetype and its gifts.

For me, this process meant attending to my body's needs during those many years I had seemingly endless viruses raging through me. It meant making a conscious decision to let go of my goals and dreams of career and wealth and relationships. I knew I just didn't have the strength or energy to fulfil them. It meant I had to take time off work, and sometimes resign from jobs because I didn't have the physical capabilities to fulfil my duties. I had to attend to my spirit and my body's needs first.

Of course, it helps immensely to have supportive structures around you, such as friends, family, counsellors and healers. These people can also be demonstrations of the Lover archetype.

But essentially, you need to bring this awareness and demonstration of love and care within yourself, first. It is, however, difficult to do it all on your own. You do need help from wiser and more experienced counsel or mentors, to help you on this journey. I certainly had this through my time with ill-health. Having access to experienced healers and energy workers enabled me to rid myself of numerous restrictive paradigms, entities and energetic patterns which were seemingly embedded in my field.

There are many courses and programs that are all about 'getting what you want'. Some call this the 'Law of Attraction' or finding the Warrior or Goddess within. For many of them, they are merely designed to glorify your wants and desires to be needed, valued and adored. Many of these programs are just pathways to narcissism and avoidance. They often ask you to imagine yourself as living a 'fantastic' lifestyle and encourage you to create goals and dreams around these inflated and grandiose imaginings.

But they don't attend to your real needs as a human being; your soul's work of healing your multi-layered and multi-dimensional Self. They don't attend to your fears and wounds, or to be of service. They don't allow you then to create ways of bringing your greatest gifts and wisdom into the world.

The loving presence that you want for yourself is not 'out there' in another relationship. It's not in some exercise regime, or a pure dietary program, or in some righteous belief system. It is not in the creation of world-saving business plans or causes. It begins with an honest and caring, loving relationship with yourself. This is very ordinary, very simple, and very powerful.

This *is* the work. It is about appreciating yourself in all your messiness, all your fears, uncertainties and woundedness. This is stepping into your vulnerability and finding the courage and power inherent in that. It is holding yourself responsible and accountable for who you are, where you are, and what you have done. It is powerful, simple, and noble work. It is *the* work that truly changes the world and liberates both you and humanity at the same time.

So, when you see a man or a woman who has been through their journey, and knows themselves truly, who has been humbled, experienced their vulnerability and emerged remembering and embodying their true magnificence and grandeur, you see someone who has integrated their Soul and Spirit in this world. This person is a joy to be around. You can sense their beauty and contentment in very ordinary environments. This is when the world and life just feel right, even if you are not getting what you want, right now.

Trying to Get Everything Right

Trying to get everything right, and living the right way, *all* the time, is very difficult.

Feeling what you feel, whatever you feel, with awareness, means you are living in the present, in 'za now'. Feeling puts you into your body, and your body is *here and now*. There is nothing wrong with feeling, even though you and others may judge certain feelings as 'positive' and others 'negative'.

Depression, sadness and apathy, for example, are natural emotions. You may experience these feelings to release and heal past trauma and woundedness. This woundedness *must* be felt for it to be cleared and transmuted. This can be extremely uncomfortable and may last for a long time.

By being present to these feelings, and allowing them to be felt *safely*, is what allows you to transcend your circumstances and attain a level of freedom and satisfaction. You achieve this by acknowledging the feeling and allowing it to pass. It's hard no doubt, often excruciating, but this is truly the way to freedom and fulfilment. Feeling leads to opening, which accesses your vulnerability, which brings in healing and growth.

Both depression and apathy are normal stages of the grief cycle. It's okay to feel them. The person who experiences these intense stages, especially if they are part of a healing process, is then acting as an alchemist's vessel, even if they don't know they are doing so at the time.

This *is* the benediction; the blessing and the sacrifice you make that fulfils your soul contracts. In going through these stages, you confer that blessing of healing, firstly upon yourself, and then upon those around you. This blessing and healing are not only conferred in the present, but also to past generations, and into the future as well. This is how an action taken in the present, literally changes experience through time. As Einstein once said, "The distinction between the past, present and future is only a stubbornly persistent illusion."

Suppressing the feelings with pharmaceuticals, meditations, positive thinking, or other avoidance strategies won't alter this necessary soul-contract. The feelings must be experienced and felt for them to be transmuted, and the healing and blessing to be brought forth. They don't need to be understood, but they do need to be felt.

I have great respect for those who have endured such difficult times and made it through with enhanced self-respect and appreciation for all. They are doing a great service to their families and community by dealing with the issues and experiences as they come up.

This is the Work. Your soul's work. It is Heroic, it is very ordinary, and it is fulfilling your life's purpose.

The Difference Between Forgiveness and Release

I found out through personal experience, the difference between forgiveness and release.

A year after I was divorced, I went through a painful emotional breakdown. It triggered layers of immense grief, sadness and shame. It was an emotionally wrenching time that lasted for well over a year.

As I was recovering and coming to terms with this great upheaval, I knew I had to face the emotional baggage of my marriage. It was the most important relationship of my life up to that point. I valued it profoundly and knew my ex-wife was one of my greatest teachers, however painful that was to acknowledge. But I also wanted to move on from that pain and heartache, and I didn't know how. The many self-development books I read at the time said, *"Write a letter of forgiveness, and send it"*. So, I started writing.

My intention was not to hurt my ex-wife or blame her, but to find a way for me to move on from what I was experiencing, enabling me to move freely into the next stage of my life. So, I started writing.

I told her about what had happened to me, and how important both she and the relationship were to me. But then I got to the part where I would say, "I forgive you for...", and I would always get stuck. I wrote about five drafts and would always stop at about the same point. And I knew, s*omething's not right here.* I just didn't know what it was or how to resolve it.

I went to a friend and spoke to her about my dilemma. I told her how I would always get stuck on, "I forgive you for...". She listened and said, "Try, I *release* you instead."

She pointed out that to release someone is to take responsibility for what is going on within *you*; for *your* feelings and actions. For example, "I release you from my anger and my resentment." In saying this, I am acknowledging and accepting *my* feelings and releasing them from me. This is a true release and the pathway to freedom.

My friend continued and said, there are two forms of forgiveness: one is to release, the other is to blame. To blame someone using forgiveness is to say, "I forgive you for hurting me, for behaving selfishly, for betraying me, and for ruining my life." You could easily substitute the word 'blame' for 'forgive' to uncover the real intention and motivation behind the statement.

I went home and rewrote the letter using the word *'release'*. I was able to write it and feel good about it. I was taking responsibility for my feelings, and I was actively releasing them from my field. I was not waiting for someone else to behave in a certain way before I could move on and feel good about myself and my life.

So, I named my feelings of anger and resentment, grief and heartache, sadness and shame, and I wrote them down in a statement and released them. I took a deep breath in, and I felt them leave over the next week or so. I felt a sense of freedom and accomplishment moving through me. I had done it. I had moved on.

Some self-development and spiritual paths urge you to practice the idea that 'nothing happened' and everything is perfect. This to me, is denying what is happening within your field. It is denying your feelings, your state of mind, what is present in your body, and what happened in your life. It is important to experience the grief cycle fully, and not bypass the discomfort with 'positive' statements and sentiments.

I have found acknowledging the feelings I have and the emotional energy I am experiencing (e-motion: energy in motion) is the way to freedom and clarity. It is acknowledging that feeling and experiencing is a normal and natural part of our human experience. It is how we live out our Soul-full lives in purposeful and fulfilling ways.

I have realised that my role in this lifetime is to *feel*. To feel it all, safely, and in doing so, I know that I am fulfilling my purpose in transmuting the energy in my field. Consequently, I have learnt how to release and let go of feelings in my body, thereby allowing the inflow of newer and more transcendent energies and vibrations into my field. Having done this process many, many times now, I know all is well. I am fulfilling my purpose. And I smile. I smile contentedly.

When My Heart Weeps

I went through a period of many years where I would weep a lot. At first, it was shocking, and then I realised that this was a natural upwelling of emotion, and it was my responsibility to allow these feelings to flow. It was my responsibility to feel them and let them flow through me. This was part of my soul's mission and purpose at that time.

These feelings did not seem to have a cause that I could identify. Paradoxically, sometimes, they did not seem to have anything to do with me at all. But they were in my system, in my field, and therefore, it was my responsibility to deal with them. This meant that when I knew these feelings and energies were building up, especially around my forehead and solar plexus, I would begin a very deliberate practice of experiencing them and releasing them. I would sit very mindfully in the chair in my room and open myself to the sensations in my body. They would come in through my body, I would experience them, and then they would leave.

This meant I would actively feel the sadness, the grief or the fear in different parts of my body. My body would tighten or convulse, often excruciatingly so, and often this would be accompanied by sadness or weeping from deep within me. Eventually, often within less than a minute, the feelings would flow through me and always leave. I realised that my body was the vehicle for the transmutation of these feelings and energies. I also knew that following this process was part of my life's purpose. It was simple, painful and profound, and I knew it was the right thing to do.

In the Paolo Coelho novel 'The Alchemist', the main character, the Boy, goes through a profound process wherein he communicates with 'the Soul of the World'. The experience I described above, was my way of doing just that. My heart wept for the pain and heartache that had accumulated within my field, through me and my ancestors throughout lifetimes. And my *destiny* was to be the vehicle for the transmuting of these metaphorical leaden energies into gold. And so, just like the 'Boy' in the story, by applying these processes in my life, *I* became 'The Alchemist' in my life, quite unknowingly.

For me, this is part of the ascension process. It is part of the relief of past hurts and wounds by transmuting their energies. This is part of a huge cycle of healing that is happening worldwide currently. Most people, both women and men, go through this process quite unconsciously. But to do so, is accessing the power of their vulnerability, and enabling themselves and others to live more freely and fully. This is how we heal the world.

Living in the Opposites

"We can talk, then, of living between the opposites. To live between means that we not only recognise opposites, but rejoice that they exist...and then live in the resonating space between them."

Robert Bly - Iron John - A Book About Men.

I read this passage just before I went off to a meditation. I was considering the polarities in our lives and how many decry the opposites, fight them, and want them banned.

Our souls have a definite path to our becoming. That is our journey. The hard part is holding the tension of the opposites and living within them.

Tension arises between who you think you should be, and who you are being at that moment. When you allow yourself to acknowledge that which is moving and present within you, then you can hold and allow for the tension between the opposites.

Popular polarised beliefs are: Only people of the right opinion should be listened to, only people who eat the right way are accepted, only people who watch the same news channels have good opinions, only people who believe in conspiracies know what's really going on! Everyone else are idiots, fools, naïve, and 'sheeples'.

Artist: Abdul Rahman Abu Baker

But yesterday I saw someone living within the polarity. I was again made aware of the courage and nobility of ordinary people doing ordinary things, in their ordinary lives.

Before the meditation, I went to a local grocery store to buy some lunch. As I was parking, I saw one of the employees preparing for their shift. This teenager, maybe sixteen or seventeen years old, was tall and thin, very pale, and looked anxious and quite sickly. "Was she a girl? Was he a boy?", I asked myself. I wasn't sure. My brain was looking for a familiar pattern of gender and couldn't find it.

I then went in and did my shopping. When I was at the check-out, I went to the counter where this pale young thing was serving. "Hello, how are you?", came the standard store greeting from Korey, with a ring of sincere cheer. And then, "Is that your lunch? That looks great. I just stuffed my face full of chocolate. Good in theory, but I'm paying for it now", he/she chuckled to me.

Korey appeared bright, cheerful and friendly, quite confident and at ease engaging with me. This is someone engaging and living in the space between the opposites, and seemingly doing well.

Korey is just a kid. They have had to come to terms with an identity that is not part of the world of polarity but rather, living and being someone in-between. They seem to have found a way to live in the world by being true to themselves, and apparently, doing so successfully.

Afterwards, I was reminded of how we give and receive blessings every day. They are done through small actions and appreciations, like Korey engaging a customer in light banter, whilst working at a local grocery store. It all helps.

Blessings are not given through yelling at someone and making them wrong and ashamed for who they are, or because they don't believe or act in the *right* ways. That's bullying, and there's nothing spiritual or Earth-changing about that. That is living as the polarising force, by defining the world through separation and disconnection, rather than through engagement and communion.

We are therefore called not just to be a being of polarisation, living only as a 'good' person, doing everything 'right' and 'knowing everything', but to engage and learn to love all of ourselves. That means, *all* of ourselves, not just the nice bits, or those parts that conform to what we think we should be.

When you deny that which is happening within you, blame others, or avoid it in myriad ways, you allow a Shadow to live and grow within you. This Shadow then holds power over you, and can manipulate you and others. It becomes a powerful polarising force.

By living between the opposites, we accept the reality of the polarities, but find a way to transcend this dimension, and thereby create a pathway to the field "out beyond ideas of wrongdoing and rightdoing", as the famous Rumi quote suggests.

Holding the tension of the opposites is the *work*. This *is* our soul's work, and it does change the world. And the more we do this work, the more we will accept each other for who we are and meet each other in that field.

What a blessed day that will be.

Healing and Wholing

Triggering old wounds of deeply personal and painful experiences from the past can be a way back into Victim circles and Wounded groups.

But now, having been down that road, many people are wanting to move into the next stage of maturity; of healing and making themselves whole.

That is, acknowledge the pain and suffering, the powerlessness and the unfairness experienced in the past, and move beyond it. These things really did happen. By acknowledging these past hurts and wounds, you demonstrate respect and thereby love, for yourself. Coming to terms with this pain is part of our soul's contract to atone, redeem and mature.

This is an essential part of your movement through your human journey and life cycle and completes your soul's mission. You must move into the final stages of your Hero's Journey, through The Return, and into maturity. You are then able to finally see and accept the gifts and wisdom of your experiences and bring them back into the world.

This is what it means, to 'bring heaven down to earth'. One of the greatest of all challenges is to release the alluring power of the wound and to engage with the depth of feeling this brings, and then move through it, into healing and appreciation.

You can stay hurt and wounded and commune with the world from there if you wish, bringing forth cynicism, bitterness and defensiveness. Or you can reconcile with your feelings and experience, and incorporate the wisdom, love, and learnings into the new being that you are becoming. In doing so, you change the world.

This healing and making yourself whole takes place through you. It is only done through you. You are the alchemist's vessel here to transmute low vibration, base and leaden motives and experiences, into the golden energy of wisdom, gratitude, and appreciation. You are the vehicle of the world's healing and transformation. It is through you. Thank you for doing your work.

We are Part of Nature, and Nature is a Part of Our Healing Journey

On the morning of October 29, 2019, I got a call from my brother with some terrible news. He told me that earlier that morning, his son had killed himself. He was only 16. He was a beautiful boy.

I remember when he was born; he had a beautiful divine glow about him that lasted at least 18 months or so. I'd seen lots of little kids and babies before, but I'd never seen a child with a glow like his, nor one that lasted so long. That *light* was his core. It's where his generosity, care, humour and love came from.

But there was so much other stuff going on within Sean. He held a lot of anger and angst, woundedness and hurt, fear and bravado, which crowded his consciousness, confusing him. And this darkness was what he had to work through. But it was just too much for him. He didn't see any other choice. Ahhhhhh... he was a beautiful boy.

Since then, quite naturally, I've been thinking a lot about my nephew and what he brought to the world. He embodied huge polarised feelings and energies that was his job in this life to reconcile.

STAGE 3: THE ROAD OF TRIALS

After the call from my brother, I was driving back home to Tweed Heads, in northern New South Wales, when I decided to make a short detour along the way. I stopped to swim at Nambucca Heads. We had a holiday trip up there when I was about twelve, and I haven't been back since. I do remember, it had a great beach. I knew I needed to immerse myself in nature and engage my feelings and the cleansing power of the ocean.

The town of Nambucca Heads is not a great attraction, but the beach... the beach is magnificent. The beach is not as big as I remembered, only about 80 metres long or so. But it has a great rocky point which ushers swells around the corner into a little cove-like beach. Small waves were coming through that day and into a deeper channel next to the rocks on the point.

It's great swimming in the ocean. The salt water and the salt air have a wonderful cleansing effect. I jumped in and swam around, feeling the movement of the water all around me. I allowed myself to wallow in the water and duck under the broken waves, feeling the tingle of the bubbles on my skin as I came to the surface. Such good fun, so enlivening, and such an important refreshing and cleansing experience for me.

A beautiful boy had died just a few hours earlier. I may have cried whilst I was swimming, I don't remember. I just remember being aware of the aliveness of the ocean; being pushed around, aware of the movement, the colours, the sounds, and the light. Ahhhh... I sighed. He was a beautiful boy.

A few days later, I lay down under a tree for a little while. I allowed myself to relax, breathe more slowly, and feel that I too, am part of nature.

I know that my beautiful nephew is alright. I know he is laughing and smiling with his spirit guides right now. But it is here that it is tough. It's hard being human. It's hard, finding and fulfilling our purpose.

This life brings hardships and confusion, great joys and great despair. We must endure a journey that challenges us to our utmost limits. And then, finally... we breakthrough, we find a way, or we don't. We find the way to reconcile with our conflicts, our stress, and our turmoil. We learn how to relax and be part of nature, rather than always trying to fight it.

I urge you too, to find a way to be with nature today. Sit in a park. Stand by a tree. Go for a swim. Commune with the birds, or just lie on the grass. It won't solve your problems, but it might just be the catalyst you need for healing and growth, enabling you to endure, and find the way through to your gifts and grace.

Go well and feel your peace.

VALE Sean Duncan Elias Harris — a beautiful boy. You are always loved and appreciated.

The Power of Listening

Listening is probably the most important and underrated health and healing practice you can do. Sometimes the best support you can give someone going through a hard time is to close your mouth and pay attention. Pay attention to what is happening for them right now?

I'm not just referring to the content of what they are saying, but also the emotion and feeling of how they are being right now. How are their energy levels and attitudes? How is their body language? Are they hunched over? Are they using particular words or symbols a lot?

This capacity to listen for feeling and energy is difficult, especially if someone is coming at you in a highly charged state. But what is the feeling underlying their upset? Are they expressing a feeling of hurt, woundedness, or a sense of betrayal, abandonment, or fear?

Many people want to immediately launch into 'fix-it' mode to get away from the uncomfortable feelings as quickly as possible. But this doesn't resolve the underlying issues which caused the emotional outburst in the first place. This is where good listening is the most courageous and powerful action you can take.

Sometimes the best thing you can do is not know the answers and not provide solutions. "I really don't know what to say for you right now. I hear your anguish and upset, but I just don't know what to do or say for you right now." This may add to the frustration of the person going through a hard time because they often are looking for someone to rescue them and solve their problems.

But mostly, people just need to know they are seen, heard, and valued whilst they go through their experiences. When someone feels heard, they feel validated and respected. This often provides the acknowledgement they were seeking in the first place. It provides that safe place to allow them to move through their emotional state and allow a more open and stable state to establish itself. From here, different solutions become available.

And listening to men is one of the most under-rated and valuable things you can do for their health and well-being. It is something that neither men nor women are very good at.

Listening is a sign of acknowledgement, appreciation, and of value; that you matter, and you matter right now. This is love in action. It is a doing word. A word of being and allowing and valuing.

When you are busy telling, fixing, blaming or abusing, you don't allow that man or woman to be who they are and what they want most; to be acknowledged, appreciated and valued right now.

Most people, men included, live unacknowledged lives of consequence, courage and nobility. I know many men who have survived lives of blame and abuse, failure and depression, isolation, and ill-health. Just listening to their story, can provide the catalyst for healing and growth.

And even though listening takes time, takes effort, and often takes you into your discomfort zone, this is the way you demonstrate *love*. Love becomes a verb by listening. Just by this simple act, you create a pathway to healing.

Perhaps this ordinary skill of listening and attending to someone is the 'super-power' you are meant to embody and demonstrate as your personal mastery and soul's gift in the world.

Questions and Exercises:

1. Give some thought as to when, where and how, 'The Road of Trials' showed up in your life.
   - Name three of these occasions. Eg: your family life, your workplace, in your health.
   - What were the gifts and the pressures this Road brought to you?
   - What archetypes did The Road of Trials bring up for you? Eg: the Hero, the Victim, the Healer, the Magical Child, the Mentor, the Rescuer, etc?
2. Looking back, what three things do you think you were supposed to learn from The Road of Trials?
3. How did you respond to the various trials and challenges you were presented? Name two that you know you responded well, and two that you know you didn't respond well.
4. What pressures were upon you to make decisions during The Road of Trials?
   - How did you make your decisions?
5. Name three things from this part of the book that moved you or struck you as important.
6. Creative expression - drawing: Take some time to find a quiet space. Breathe deeply and relax your body. Feel the breath go all the way through your body, and clear your mind. With paper, coloured pencils or crayons in front of you, ask yourself clearly, "Show me what is important for me to know from this part of the book."

   Then, with your non-dominant hand, choose a pencil or crayon, and start drawing. It doesn't matter what it looks like, just create. Change hands when your body tells you. Repeat.

Stage 4:
The Abyss

The Hero (You) continues their Journey in this new world. They acquire skills and knowledge that enables them to achieve success and competence in this world. However, no worthwhile journey is easy. The Hero finds that old methods don't work anymore. They encounter perils and hardships on the path to their growth, discovery and self-realisation.

Pressure builds as major obstacles confront you. Imminent dangers appear to the livelihood and personal safety of the Hero. It appears that all hope is lost. You are taken on a journey into the dark reaches of your heart, mind and soul. It is the ultimate test and ordeal.

The Hero enters the Abyss.

Artist: Shapelined, Sheki, Azerbaijan

The Power and Importance of the Abyss

The Abyss brings forth powerful archetypes and profound issues for you to deal with. The Destroyer is the most powerful force through this time. It must come through during this stage. It must.

If you are consciously aware of its presence, you can prepare yourself by allowing its flow. Or you can resist its power by exerting your will by putting up barriers, shutting down, bypassing or disconnecting from life. Either way, it will emerge into your life, and it will clear out and purge you of patterns or things that are not aligned with the next stage of your life.

Nature does this too of course. It may do so harshly or incrementally, but environments are changed through natural forces every day. The features of a coastline can change dramatically over time through the power and constant movement of tides and waves. Forests, especially mono-cultural forests, will sometimes experience infestations of bugs or disease that wipes out whole stands of trees.

In Australia, the Destroyer manifests every year through bush fires. But what happens very quickly, often within a few days after the fire, is that new life comes back to the forest. On the harshly blackened trunks and branches of the trees, brand new, baby green shoots emerge. It is astonishing to see. Out of devastation and destruction, new life is birthed.

In your life, the Destroyer archetype will affect you in your relationships, finances, health, career or social status at some point. You may suffer loss, betrayal, a campaign against you, illness or an accident. But all these painful life events, as inconvenient as they are, are all part of your journey into releasing old identities, beliefs and patterns. This is so that new patterns, talents and awarenesses can emerge and arise.

But before this new creative force can come in, there must be a clearing of space within you for new seeds to germinate and grow. This is the purpose of the purge and the blackening; you cannot have a new beginning, without first going through the ending.

So, finding the way to work with this natural stage of life, of tension, distress and destruction, will move you into a much more creative, open and abundant state of being. You will then walk into the most creative and fulfilling time of your life.

STAGE 4: THE ABYSS

Physical Hardships on Your Journey

Part of your Hero's Journey is to go through periods of extreme physical, mental, emotional and spiritual hardship. The purpose of which is for you to experience profound transformation through a complete recalibration and reorientation of your senses and worldview.

Artist: Karmie Varya, Saint Mary Magdalene

The Journey does this by giving you trials and challenges that move you into fields of discomfort and adversity, that test you to your utmost limits. It is only when you reach these limits, and are pushed beyond them, that you can access and finally release deeply held beliefs, wounds and identities. This process is an opening, which then leads to an emptying and purging of your body and soul. It is only when you are empty, when you allow a vacuum to be created, that nature can, of its own accord, and in its own timing, seed this barren landscape with new life.

This is the active role of the Destroyer and then the Creator in your life.

On my journey, I have experienced this stage many times. In 2008, I experienced the first of thirteen fainting spells that I can remember. The last one was in late 2013. All of them were extremely stress-filled and wrenching experiences that strained my body, mind and spirit to its limits.

The first time it happened, I had been ill with a body-sapping virus for at least a month. I was fatigued, physically weak and constantly sweating and cold. My body was slow and heavy as if my blood flowed like glue through it. I had had viruses of some sort continually since 2004, and I was sick of being sick.

At the time, I was coming to terms with the final stage of my application to the priesthood within the Jesuit Order of the Catholic Church. I was confronted with the final threshold I needed to cross to formally apply. It was not a path I wanted. I was not 'following my bliss' as Joseph Campbell would say. But it was a path I knew I had to walk. It was my *calling*. And my calling was clear. Many signs confirmed that this was so. This was my path and I knew it to be so. To fulfil this soul contract, I had to walk this path, and I had to follow it to its conclusion.

So, whilst I was sick with viruses and coming to terms with this momentous life-changing decision, I fainted. It was sometime late in the night or early morning in November. I got up, however unsteadily, to go to the toilet. I felt slightly nauseous at the time which was different than normal. As I got to the toilet, my discomfort increased and I was aware that I might vomit, and so I got on my knees readying myself. Then I fainted. It was sudden and unexpected, and coming back into consciousness was one of the most horrible and terrifying experiences I have ever had.

I became aware that I was lying on the floor and that I couldn't move freely. My head was rushing and roaring with sound. My eyes were open, but I couldn't see. There were images rushing through my head, moving so furiously that I couldn't grasp anything. The sound, the sight and the feeling in my body were terrifying. I was completely overwhelmed by the sensations. I was aware that I was screaming. It was the only response I could make to being so overwhelmed and out-of-control. Many, many images were streaming through my consciousness at a great pace. I couldn't hold onto any one of them. I couldn't focus on anything. I knew I was sweating and cold, and I was aware that I was screaming and screaming at this terrifying experience of loud, rushing sensations of overwhelm.

Then slowly, so horribly slowly, the sensations moved through and abated. Slowly focus returned to my sight. I was able to gather my awareness of where I was. I had fallen beside the toilet and my head was lying at the dusty base. As embarrassed as I was of my position, I moved as best I could around to the front. My screams slowed and became calmer as my breathing moved into rasping gasps and moans. I was confused, dazed, and overwhelmed by what had just happened. After a while, I was able to find some degree of calm, but then my body took over again.

My body needed to purge. I expelled everything within me, harshly. I retched again and again. Eventually, thankfully, the purge ended. There was nothing more for my body to get rid of, and I slumped exhausted by the toilet wall. Slowly, I was able to crawl a few metres to a carpeted area near the kitchen, and I lay there, absolutely wretched and exhausted, sweating, cold, isolated and alone. I don't know how long I lay there, but eventually, I regained some control over my breathing and my body, and I was able to stagger my way back to my bedroom.

Utterly exhausted, I collapsed onto my bed. I drew up the pillows, gathered my doona around me, and sweating, cold and utterly defeated, I allowed myself to relax into where I was right then.

As I was lying there, my brother's words from years before came back to me, "Why don't you just see if you can enjoy being sick?" Inexplicably, I started laughing. I laughed at the absurdity of my circumstances. There was nothing I could do. My body was working with its intelligence under its command to do its own thing; I was but a passenger and my body the vehicle for this process.

This was the first of about thirteen similar experiences which occurred over the next few years. However, where this first one was undoubtedly harsh and horrible, it seemed benign in retrospect. The subsequent episodes, however, were not so. They became more intense and more pervasive in my life.

For months in 2011 and 2012, I experienced constant nausea, feelings of stress and even symptoms of shock as it felt like darker forces were behind my experiences. I felt like there was a dark energetic force intervening in my life to strike at me and incapacitate me through my body. It was a debilitating and harsh time to move through. But eventually, so achingly slowly, I did.

In October 2013, I experienced my final fainting episode. This time it was triggered by a physical jarring in my body.

The windows in my bedroom were spring-loaded and one of them was open. It was around eleven o'clock at night and I was lying in bed when the wind picked up and I moved to close the window. I got up and adjusted the window, when my hands slipped and the window smashed down onto my thumbs. I cried out as I felt the rush of sharp pain through my hands and into my head. It really hurt. I also knew that this was exactly the sort of thing that would trigger a fainting attack and the subsequent debilitation. I prepared myself and it came upon me quickly.

The experience was similar to previous times with the horrible and terrifying intensity of coming back into consciousness. Because of my previous experience, I was able to look after myself well and managed to return to bed within about forty minutes or so. As usual, it took about a full day and a half to recover from such an extreme experience.

A few days later, I had a healing session with a friend who works in shamanic practices. I needed to clear my energy field of any dark forces and entities which could manipulate me seemingly so easily and effectively. The window smashing on my thumbs was just the sort of shuddering experience that would open a hole in my field so they could come in and manipulate me further. Thankfully, the healing session sewed up the holes in my field and expelled any remaining dark forces and entities. It felt so good knowing that that episode was at an end.

But then later that year, on December 22nd I experienced another shocking event. The week prior I had been invited by a friend to house-sit his place in a beautiful small town just north of Byron Bay in New South Wales. It was a wonderful opportunity and a great way to spend Christmas and New Year celebrating the completion of old cycles and the opening to the new, in a beautiful and comfortable environment.

That morning, I was riding my bike back to the railway station after having given a sound meditation session. It had just been raining, and I was going a little too fast as I turned down a side street. My front wheel hit some gravel and slid out from under me. I crashed heavily in the next instant. My face hit the road, breaking my glasses, and sending them off my face and onto the road. Both my hands hit the road hard, scraping and cutting them severely. The handlebars twisted around and pushed heavily into my left side causing intense bruising. I groaned in pain at the quickness and sharpness of the accident. I was aware enough to know that I had to get off the road as quickly as I could. In pain, I gathered up my bike and hobbled over to the grassed verge on the side of the road. On my knees, I rued what had just happened, and I knew this was exactly the sort of harsh jolting experience that would bring on another fainting episode. So, I waited on the grass, in pain, holding myself for the inevitable further shock to my system.

But then, something different happened. Within a minute a bystander came up to me to attend to my needs. She enquired how I was and could see I was in pain. I realised I was not isolated this time. Then someone else came along, and soon brought out some bandages and some frozen peas to put on my hands. I was being looked after. I was still waiting for the shock to kick in and the usual routine of me fainting and then vomiting. Someone offered me some water. And still nothing. Soon after that I started laughing. You know, those times when something hurts so much you start laughing?

After about five minutes or so the shock did come. And I thought, *okay here we go, fainting and vomiting time*. I was waiting for the usual intensity to build up to extreme discomfort, then the fainting, and then the vomiting. But it didn't come. The shock came into my body, and then slowly eased out again after about forty seconds or so. I was left feeling surprised, incredibly relieved and even elated. I was still in pain and I was still smiling and laughing. It wasn't coming anymore. It had gone from my system. I was just going to experience pain and nothing else. I was so relieved. The entities were gone. And oh, I felt like singing out 'Hallelujah! Hallelujah brothers and sisters. Hallelujah!'

Within fifteen minutes of the accident I accepted a lift home from the neighbour, who put my bike in his car. I thanked him and the others for helping me so quickly and effectively. I was holding my hands wrapped in frozen peas on one side and mixed vegetables on the other, and I was smiling. I felt incredibly grateful. And oh, it bloody hurt. My hands really hurt.

I smiled and smiled as I got home and lay down on my bed to attend to my wounds. I laughed, and I think I may have cried from gratitude. I knew that a harrowing chapter of my life was completed. It had ended and I was free. I was finally free.

This last episode heralded a new appreciation of my life's journey. It affirmed my belief that I was being guided and looked after. I was exhausted and elated, and naturally needed time for rest and recuperation.

In the new year, I was able to get a part-time job, and had extended periods of casual work which enabled me both to rest and provide resources enough for me to survive. But more than that, I had a growing sense of ease and confidence within myself and my relationship with the world. I had a greater appreciation for the journey I had been on. I realised that I had finally completed a huge and important cycle in my life. I had completed a full Hero's Journey cycle, and I was now preparing for the next stage.

And so, began the next stage: the challenge of Integration.

Taking the plunge – Going to Depth

There are times when we can't help it, we must go to depth. As much as we may resist or use well-worn avoidance strategies, like blame or sex and drugs, or meditation, or work, we must go to depth.

Artist: Janrye

Life calls us into these circumstances so we can experience more of ourselves and uncover more of our true character and nature.

When this call to depth comes, we may feel totally overwhelmed, totally victimised and that life is unfair. And yet we must endure and go through it.

It can come through tragedy, heartache, the pressure of work or the calling of our soul. Whatever the stimulus, this pressured situation is calling us to go to our depths. It is calling us to experience and explore feelings and senses that we may have never experienced before or have long suppressed or repressed. And we experience it alone.

This experience, as uncomfortable as it may be, is there to help us grow into a new self; to create a new structure within and around us.

This means that familiar patterns will be disrupted; in relationships, career, money, where we live, etc. It must be disrupted so the old can leave, and so the new has space to plant it seeds and grow.

We must experience this fall into depth; this fall into uncertainty. We must fall into the unknown and be moved by forces that are beyond our control. We then become aware that we cannot control our environment anymore. And it's not our fault.

But we always have a choice. Our choice is not in what we experience, but how we experience it. We can experience this uncertainty with terror, anger and blame, or we can experience the same circumstances with acceptance and a sense of peace.

Even though we may experience feelings of sadness, fear, depression and powerlessness, we have a choice as to how we experience these feelings; with resentment, resistance and defensiveness, or with acceptance, self-love and appreciation.

Men especially, need to be encouraged and feel safe to go to these places of depth. There is a reason why male suicide is so high, it is because they feel isolated and unsafe.

Through my passage into depth, I am now able to put my hand on my heart and allow the love and appreciation I have for myself and my journey, to permeate through me into a sense of joy and acceptance. I am alright, and I know I am loved.

Your Body Is More Honest Than You Will Ever Be

Your body is more honest than you will ever be. It has greater intelligence than you know. Let your body be your guide on your healing journey.

Having a disciplined practise that engages your body, like Qigong, Tai Chi or yoga, is essential as you go through change.

Practices that engage and harmonise your breath and your body, through movement, absolutely enhance your ability to cope and engage with change. It enables you to honour and serve your body, mind, and soul.

It enables you to be open and engaged with the forces within you and those outside of you, so you can remain grounded and present with what is happening.

It enables you to trust yourself, and trust that your soul is guiding you and directing you to the people and places you need to be right now. This is the true meaning of the Law of Attraction.

And being part of a community of friends or groups that are also committed to walking into their higher potential and embodying it, supports, nurtures, and inspires you on your Hero's journey, in all its challenges and achievements.

The Gift of Illness

The gift of being really ill is that it brings your attention and actions back very close to you. When you are ill, your attention is quite literally from here to the toilet, from here to the bucket, or from here to the kitchen or bathroom. Your attention and focus become basic and simple; they come very close to you. Your body is leading the way. It has an intelligence that just *knows*, better than you think.

During these times of illness, you don't have the attention or the energy for all those other important things like projects, careers, or even relationships. They seem far away. Your attention becomes focussed on simply attending to your most basic bodily needs and requirements. That's all.

Afterwards, it may appear that these extreme moments are part of a grand plan to create change in your life; to change habits of thought, perception, and priorities. We have all heard people who have survived critical illnesses say that this 'was the best thing that ever happened to me'.

At a soul level, if you are someone who has, through lifetimes, put other people's needs and desires before your own, then, to break this cycle and to get your attention back to valuing and appreciating yourself, your soul may work through your body, and give you an illness. You may need to purge all that is in your body, to in effect, reset and recalibrate your system to put yourself first. Your body's intelligence does this extreme action in order to create an environment so uncomfortable, that the old toxins must either be expelled or die. You cannot remain the same after this.

After this extreme experience, you will literally feel emptier, and often clearer in your thoughts and energy than before. The physical toxins may have cleared through your body, and it is also likely that other psychic and emotional energies have also been cleared from your system.

Because of this purging and emptying, many people experience an awakening to a new awareness of themselves, life and the world. This is a powerful experience that initiates you into a new state of being. It is a harsh way in which you can become aware of your soul's purpose. Afterwards, you may refocus your priorities and attention to activities that are more aligned with this awareness and purpose.

As you come out of this extreme emptying stage, there are always temptations to go back to the old ways of living and being. But your ability to discern the difference between what is distracting you and taking you off track, and that which is aligned with your true path, is now heightened, and enhanced.

The temptations will look like demands from jobs, projects or relationships that put 'time-bound' and 'scarcity-based' pressures on you to comply or extend yourself beyond your capacity. You will sense that something just doesn't feel right.

So then, each time you consciously attend to your body's needs, you demonstrate respect, love and care to yourself. You enrich yourself, even just a little bit. And with each little step and action of care and respect to yourself, you become stronger, more healed, more content and more able to live openly, fully and lovingly in your world. You become the change in the world, because of an illness.

Soul Contracts - a Profound Agreement

> Only in silence the word,
> Only in dark the light,
> Only in dying life:
> Bright the hawk's flight
> On the empty sky.
> **— From Tales of Earthsea, by Ursula K. Le Guin**

Freedom comes not from avoiding and distracting yourself from the things you need to do and experience in your life, but from having the courage and discipline to feel, do what you *need* to in your life. This means being aware of and attending to your *soul contracts.*

Soul contracts are those agreements you have made prior to your birth; to experience and learn certain things and apply particular virtues in your life. This means prior to your birth, your soul decided to be in your birth family, be in relationship with certain people, or it could be completing or healing intergenerational issues, experiencing illness, or freeing yourself from karmic patterns or untrue beliefs.

Soul contracts aren't just with people or circumstances, they also relate to archetypal issues that you need to deal with such as wealth and poverty, freedom and empowerment, creativity and abundance, discipline and control, power and trust. These are all big, powerful issues and energies which you must experience and reconcile within your lifetime.

So how do you work with these big issues and resolve them in your lifetime?

First, listen to the voice of your intuition. Do what this little voice says. This intuitive voice is still, quiet and certain. It is clear. It emanates clarity. There is no emotion, just *knowing*. Listening to your intuition often means spending more time closing your mouth and opening your ears, than it does in talking, telling or thinking. This is demonstrating respect by listening rather than telling. As illustrated in, 'Only in silence the word'. Only in your silence, do you receive the gift.

The next two lines, 'Only in dark the light, only in dying life', is about walking your path, even if it leads into the Abyss of darkness and death. It is here that you must acknowledge and then embrace your own dark and shadow.

Only by journeying through the place of your greatest darkness, bringing forth your greatest fears, wounds and feelings, do you encounter the light. Only through experiencing those times of your utmost grief, where you are bereft of hope, in the death you experience through failure, do you move into a new life. It is only in the dark, that you will find the light.

New life appears again, often from completely unexpected areas, and in its own time. This is the natural flow of the season of winter in your life, the Destroyer archetype and the earth force.

Temptations often arrive just before you accept your greatest gifts. This is where someone or circumstances will come along to lure you back to your previous life. This could be a relationship, or job, which takes you back to your old ways, habits and perceptions, or the temptation of money, sex or status.

But your path to the *new* is definite. You are given these temptations and distractions to force you into a decision which defines your values and your sense of self. And when you make that decision, you experience freedom: 'Bright the hawk's flight, on the empty sky.'

It is through facing the things you really don't want to, but that you need to, that you grow and evolve to experience and embody your greatest freedom; to fly on into the next great moment of potential.

The poem is a simple and humbling image of the movement into awareness and enlightenment. It embraces the paradox of polarity, that you can only gain your true self by letting go of everything. That by losing everything, you gain it all.

And after this ordeal and initiation, only then you will fly in a completely new and empty space... 'bright the hawk's flight on the empty sky.' You experience the freedom of the new.

The Humbling

Your journey to self-appreciation always begins with a humbling. This breakdown inevitably leads you to a breakthrough.

Your soul's purpose is not just in your outward achievements, but mostly in your healings and learnings. It is in the times that you break open, that you create the acknowledgement and appreciation of *all* the unaccepted parts of yourself; the fragments that you have ignored or blocked and live in Shadow.

As this humbling occurs, you do the profound work of bringing the disparate parts of your Self together in your embrace. This is healing. This is making yourself whole. And this *is* the change you want to see in the world because *you* become that change. It is through your experience of healing, that you heal the world.

It is instructive to know that *humbling* and *humility* come from the word 'humus' meaning the organic component of earth or soil. It is created by the decomposition and breaking down of other organic material.

Experiencing *humility* then is the act of bringing you 'down to earth', to get your body close to the earth from which all matter comes from. This is what being grounded means. It is through the breaking down of what was previously known and certain, that the new form and new being can emerge.

This is why, when you are humbled, you fall to your knees and place your head and your heart on the floor. You are surrendering. You are surrendering all that you once were and believed yourself to be, to the earth.

You are symbolically re-joining the earth, becoming one with where your body came from, and to where it will return. It is an acknowledgement that everything must grow from the ground up.

Thank you for doing your work, it is profound.

A Breakdown Is Essential for A Breakthrough

Accepting the necessity and the uncomfortable nature of the work of transformation moves you further into alignment with the natural cycles of life, and the way of the divine feminine. Western society has not worked in this way well at all. It has judged these states of being as weak and negative and a failure.

But a breakdown in our emotional or physical state is important, in that it breaks down the protective armour and barriers that you have created to ensure your survival and success in this world. It means that the intense energy required to keep everything under control and protected, comes to its natural limits.

However, these protective patterns are essential for your survival. They help you stay safe and give you a feeling of security, control, or success, for a while anyway. These patterns and armoury include false beliefs, denial, defensiveness and avoidance strategies.

But eventually, as you continue your journey into maturity, these patterns cannot stand. Eventually, you must let them go as they do not serve your greater purpose, and the weight of your armour and avoidance patterns eventually, will become overwhelming.

These patterns could be your goals, such as business, vocation, relationship, lifestyle, controlling your circumstances or being successful and revered. Some may be realistic, but others may be fantasies and illusions. This is illustrated in The Heroine's Journey as identification with the masculine, or outward achievement and seeking external forms of success and validation.

But as your soul calls you to your growth and destiny, these patterns of defence and avoidance, must break down. They must. This stage is essential for your breakthrough into a new life and new ways.

It is a hard path for sure, but ultimately, your breakdown is the way that the light of your higher self comes to illuminate more of yourself. This breakdown creates a pathway of opening to your self-appreciation, growth and freedom. It is a breakdown into your vulnerability and the undiscovered power that lies there.

This is the benefit of the trials and challenges we go through. They provide the opportunity for an Initiation into releasing and burning off the accumulated burdens of outdated beliefs, defences and armour that you have carried all your life. It allows you to descend into your depths and reclaim your true divine nature by finally allowing you to meet and embrace yourself fully. This Initiation then allows you to embrace and join with all the dispirit parts of yourself and give thanks. You have healed and you have made yourself whole again. Truly a courageous life journey.

Does Rock Bottom Teach Us More Than Living on a Mountaintop?

Going to desperate depths and going to great heights are both natural pathways of your journey.

Mountaintops teach you about perspective and gaining a holistic worldview. They teach you about the wonderful and often ecstatic feelings of joy, love and high vibrational light that you experience in high states of spiritual awareness. These are rich and beautiful feelings, something to be savoured for sure. The experience helps you expand into the infinite capacity of light and energy that is within this multi-dimensional universe.

But going to mountaintops and seeking high spiritual truths, can also lead to the way of grandiosity and disconnection from the earth and your earthly life. It can lead to arrogance and pomposity by being consumed by a sense of purity and sanctity. Many spiritual people become overly judgemental of those who don't live up to these high (impossible) standards and expectations.

Eventually, even those who live on mountaintops must travel down into the valleys and engage with the world. This is a normal part of your life's journey, and part of this journey is to experience a *fall*.

The *fall* is not a condemnation, but rather the process of humbling that enables your spirit to move out of the world of *high light* (living in purity and sanctity) and come down into the world of earth and Soul. This process of literally bringing you 'down to earth', is where illness, failure and breakdown become the catalysts for your healing and growth, by opening you to your vulnerability.

Old ways that worked on the mountaintop don't work down here on earth. This is where you experience loss to your 'rock bottom', which brings up deep-seated feelings you may not have known were there: guilt, shame, abandonment, fear, anger, rage and resentment. You are now engaging with the deep levels of the hidden power within the earth and your Soul, and you must do it. This is walking and fulfilling your soul's path.

As you emerge from this process of *falling* into blackness and disintegration, you re-establish yourself anew in the world. At first, you may be fearful and uncertain as to how to set your feet solidly in the world again. But slowly, you do emerge, as if a new being, into the world again.

It is this process that truly teaches you about the cycles and holism of your life's journey. It is through this journey from up on high, to down low, that you gain compassion and love for yourself and others. You learn how to value the courage it takes to live an ordinary life in this world, and value the journey that got you to this place of appreciation.

Spending Time with Yourself

Spending time with yourself, being alone, is one of the most healthful things you can do, especially in times of great personal challenge and change.

Being alone also allows the great healing energies, those great natural forces, to come into your body and your consciousness, and do their work of clearing old wounds, grief and perceptions. This is deep work. This is the work of self-care and healing.

This work can be truly profound. It can be extremely uncomfortable to feel your feelings, especially if these feelings have gone unacknowledged for most, if not all of your life. For many, this was because it wasn't safe for you to experience them as a child. You may have therefore created defensive patterns and habits that have ruled your thoughts and behaviours for most of your life.

This can lead to an addiction to stress and distraction; to constantly be doing, thinking, and planning. *"What's the next thing I need to do? Who do I need to contact? Who am I if I am not doing or achieving the next thing?"*

By constantly being in this state of activity and anxiety, you do not allow any time or space for yourself to feel your underlying sense of self, your intuition, or your *calling*. To *not* feel then becomes the goal. It becomes a primary act of defence, resistance, and safety.

There is an underlying fear guiding this behaviour and sense of self. A fear of loss and not being good enough. There is a profound fear of facing inner beliefs of worth and value and empowerment. A fear that if you stand still, then everything will be taken away from you, things will fall apart, and you will be abandoned, shamed, and rejected. It is a primal fear.

But spending time alone, or with someone who can hold you during this time of emptiness, breaks down those barriers. It allows you to experience the truth of those beliefs... that they are all false. It allows you to face the denials you practice that keep this false world running. It provides the space and time for you to put down your swords and shields and dissolve the armour you have spent so long strengthening and honing.

For some, this breakdown of falsity is the very thing they are running away from. "If I stay busy, busy, busy, in projects, in causes, in relationships, in working for my business, in building or creating something... then I will be safe! I won't be a loser, and I won't be alone." This is truly the time to step into your vulnerability.

But there is a big process going on. You are not the only one. There is a natural force of change moving through many people across the world. This change is challenging you to leave behind the old structure of beliefs, patterns and identities that kept you safe throughout your life. It is deeply challenging to spend time with yourself and let go of that old unhealthful structure and energetic system that has lived within your field all your life.

But as you learn how to feel more deeply and truly, you create space for a new structure based on appreciation, gratitude and inner-referencing. These qualities become your new foundations and are the pathway to healing. From here, you engage and interact with the world in a completely different way.

Now is a time to appreciate the wondrous, gutsy, courageous, and brilliantly noble being that is You. You have survived, and spending time with your Self, enables and expands feelings of self-trust and self-respect. This then radiates out into the world, creating new outcomes and experiences for you and others.

So, spend some time today and say, "Thank you" to yourself, for going on your journey and bringing your gifts and true Self into the world, for the benefit of all.

The Return of the Prodigal Son - The Hero's Journey in a Painting

'The Return of the Prodigal Son' by Rembrandt Harmenszoon van Rijn, is a magnificent painting and represents a beautiful and powerful human story. It is a parable of our journey through life, from advantage and support, to humiliation and humbling. Who hasn't walked this road? I know I have, many, many times.

It is a picture highlighting the most powerful human drama. It shows three main characters and their relationship to one another: the old decrepit Father, the young, humbled son, and the older brother/Warrior.

The picture depicts the time when the son returns home after failing in his ventures to achieve success in a new life and having spent all the inheritance that was given to him before he left. He returns, on his knees, humiliated, ashamed, and despairing, in poverty and hopelessness. He has nothing. His once fine colourful clothes are now rags; filthy and brown, blending with the earth.

He is welcomed, joyously by his aged, blind and decrepit father. They are joined together as one. The father's hands embrace his young son, in an act of compassion and care, one hand on his son's back, over his heart, and the other, his guiding hand, on his son's shoulder. The son is shown, enfolded and nestled into the heart and belly of his father, craving his father's forgiveness, comfort and love.

In stark contrast, is the posture and position of the elder brother. He is pictured as aloof and separate from the other two. He stands stiffly, enclosed by his cloak and positioned two steps above them, looking down upon them, with an attitude of disdain and cold judgement.

STAGE 4: THE ABYSS

Artist: Rembrandt Harmenszoon van Rijn,
Return of the Prodigal Son

In the parable, the elder brother is cast as resenting the compassion and generosity shown to his younger brother. He says to his father, "Behold, these many years I have served you, and I never disobeyed a commandment of yours, but you never gave me a goat…" (Luke 15:29–30). He is expressing his sense of righteous entitlement to his father. Having done *all* the right things throughout his life, always been *good*, always followed the rules and lived righteously, he feels he has never been rewarded or appreciated for this good behaviour.

I find this painting very illustrative of our times. I know I have been all three of these characters in my life, and I see them demonstrated in the world today. I know I have been the arrogant, judgemental and emotionally distant character, enclosed by a cloak of my righteously held beliefs. And I know many others are the same.

I know I have been the humbled and humiliated younger son, ashamed at having lost everything, again.

I also know I have been the compassionate, welcoming Father character too, embracing those who are travelling a difficult road, seeing their hardship and valuing their journey.

I have seen over the last twenty years or so, a great movement into righteousness, entitlement, fundamentalism and polarity throughout cultures around the world. These are all aspects of the growth of the ego; the desire to control outcomes, control behaviour and control beliefs. We can see this in common attitudes towards the environment, social behaviours, dietary choices, exercise regimes, political beliefs and of course, religious beliefs.

Many people have become the elder brother character. They are judgemental, conceptual, ideological, puritanical, entitled and distant. They feel more comfortable in the binary world of polarising beliefs and attitudes, like judging and blaming, than they do in bringing a loving embrace to others, like the Father.

But to me, the real change in the world comes from the loving, compassionate and humbling embrace of the Father and the Son. Both are enriched by this encounter. One has lost all his finery, stripped away to his barest essentials. The other, the Father, the King/Queen archetype, comes down to meet his son at this most basic level. He too is humbled in his physical presence; he is old and infirm. But this is where true change occurs: in the heart and embrace of kindness and compassion.

The Wounded Healer – The Gift of Suffering

Most of the greatest healers experience the grief cycle in all its messiness, disruption and torture. They emerge from this journey with wisdom, compassion and a sense of ease with which they can engage the world. They become mature emanations of a loving and expansive humanity.

They have experienced personally, that life and the world *are* unfair. It is true. It is naturally so. Bad things happen to good people. Good things happen to bad people. There is injustice. This is just the way it is. But now what? How do you respond? How does a Healer respond?

Some people launch campaigns of blame, anger and conspiracy, as if this will change the world and make it a better place. They project guilt and shame onto others who are not behaving and thinking the *right* way. Does this work? Does this make the world a better and more beautiful place? No. No, it doesn't. Even these expressions of venting pent-up emotional energies, and directing them out at others, doesn't satisfy.

Honestly, if righteousness and condemnation were all it took to change the world and make it a better place, surely, we'd be living in Eden by now, no? Isn't several thousand years of guilting and shaming people enough?

These highly-charged emotional expressions are certainly part of the grief cycle (from Elisabeth Kübler-Ross); that is, denial and anger.

And those destined to be healers experience the grief cycle, many times throughout their lives. They too will move through all the various stages of the grief cycle, into depression and bargaining, and finally into acceptance.

That is, they may bargain with their circumstances by trying to be *good* or get everything *right*, or judge or control others to fulfil their desires. And in failing to control their circumstances and achieve their hoped-for outcomes, they experience depression. But even this isn't enough. Even this doesn't satisfy.

Eventually, they experience an awareness of the limitations of their bargaining and depression, which leads them inevitably to become accountable and responsible for how they feel, where they are, and what they are doing. This is not the same as blaming themselves or someone else. This process leads to an expansion of themselves by looking in the mirror and going to their depths. This is moving into their vulnerability and their inherent wisdom, and is the pathway to self-trust, self-referencing, self-respect and maturity.

Through this process, they change their behaviour and attitudes, and learn to appreciate themselves and their journey. They move to the place where they can apologise to those they have hurt in their past or present. This is Atonement, and one of the most courageous, formidable, and empowering stages on the Hero's Journey. It is truly the place of alchemy and change. It is the place of humbling. It is atoning for the mistakes they have made, and in doing so, preparing the way for their new path.

I admire greatly those who have experienced suffering and emerged with compassion and appreciation for themselves and the world. They truly create a change that evolves the world.

It is not the righteous that do so. It cannot be. This is because righteousness is only one part of the grief cycle: the anger stage.

To really change the world, you must complete the whole cycle, and emerge with wisdom, patience and compassion for all. This is the gift of the Wounded Healer and the path of the courageous vulnerable.

Valuing the Vulnerability of Men

Valuing vulnerability is not something Western society does very well. Historically, we value the stoic and the Warrior, not someone who openly understands, experiences and appreciates their vulnerability, their feminine side.

Many women also, as outlined in The Heroine's Journey, are trained to become Warrior women and become hardened and armoured against this aspect of themselves. The first stage of the Heroine's Journey speaks of separation or rejection of the feminine, and a movement to identify with the masculine. In doing so, the pathway to the power and worth of vulnerability is cut off, both to women and men.

Accordingly, men's emotional and spiritual need to engage with their vulnerable core is often ignored, downplayed or disparaged as not being acceptable for a man to experience. Hence, unmet emotional needs may become depressions, storms, or outwardly and inwardly destructive behaviours. And for many, an ending of their lives. My nephew and my maternal grandfather are among these men.

Artist: H. Kopp Delaney

But when you are with someone who can hold you whilst you go through difficult times, that is truly when the healing occurs. They provide a grounding stone of objectivity, curiosity and empathy. This person is best if they are slightly removed from you, like a therapist or a counsellor, rather than your lover, family member or best friend. Whoever they are, it is especially important that they don't get caught up in the emotional expression, but provide the space for you to be heard. This doesn't happen very often for men. There is often no safe place for them to be listened to, and for them to unburden themselves of their fears and anxieties.

One reason for men's isolation then, is that it is *not* safe for them to move into their vulnerability, to express their feelings, their fears or their anxieties... anywhere.

I have been in men's groups where that space has been the only safe place these men have ever experienced in their lives. They have never felt safe in their life! These could be men in their 20s, 30s, 50s or even 70s, and they have never felt safe in their life. Hence, they live within a structure based on survival. They close off, shut down, and seek distractions and ways to avoid what is going on within themselves. They don't know how to feel or express themselves safely.

And, it's hard for many women to listen to a man display his heartfelt feelings and vulnerability. They have experienced their own times of unsafety, grief and deep woundedness. They don't want him to express his fear, doubt and uncertainty. This is called 'complaining'. They want him to 'man-up' and 'step-up and 'grow-up'. They don't want him to go into his depth and find his personal power. They want him to be the man *they* want him to be, the one who will make *them* feel safe, rather than the man who is right in front of them right now.

This is showing the limitations of the patriarchal system that humanity has lived through for several thousand years now. It is a system of separating from, and devaluing and rejecting the feminine (that is, natural cycles and movements, emotions and Being). And it is about the identification, embracing and excessive importance given to the masculine (outward achievement, striving, protecting and Doing).

What so often happens in relationships is that during the times of venting and blaming, there is a diminishment and dismissing of the value of the other. Arguments bring forth high states of emotion. When directed at a man, his efforts and presence, even his manhood are dismissed as completely worthless, ineffectual and not good enough. Hence, he isolates himself even more and doesn't share what is going on within him. He isolates to protect his self-esteem and self-worth. It is not safe to be here. It is not safe.

The strength and beauty in relationships come from being with someone who can hold you whilst you are going through your natural stage of vulnerability. It is a test for them as well, as their own fears and wounds may be triggered.

It calls upon your willingness to do the work and apply this work in 'za now', as Eckhart Tolle would say. This is how you grow. These are the tests you were brought here to experience and learn from. This is part of the Journey, venturing into your vulnerability and bringing that experience into the world. This is courageous and heroic, and it is very ordinary.

Finding the avenues for self-acceptance and acknowledgement of what is going on within you is a sign of self-love. This is what heals the world. Finding someone who can provide strategies and a process to work through to this place of self-acceptance, enables you to live with a sense of safety and ease. It is very important to know that you are not alone and that accessing your vulnerability is an essential pathway to uncovering and discovering your inherent power, creativity and self-worth. Go well.

The Gifts and Burdens of Women: A Heroine's Journey

I had lunch with a woman friend of mine a while ago who said, "You know, women get emotional. They just do. And it's surprising how defensive they get when you tell them that."

So, why the defensiveness? What's wrong with getting emotional? Who or what are women protecting themselves from?

There is obviously a perceived threat. A defensive barrier comes up, and the body and the mind move into survival mode.

One of the great gifts and burdens women carry is emotion. Women do get emotional. It is their gift to allow emotion to move through them so fully and completely, that they transmute these emanations of undigested trauma and woundedness, for the collective good of us all. This is true alchemy.

Artist: Katia Honour

This is a huge task and process for the soul, for which there is very little understanding and support, even amongst women.

Men do the same thing, they experience emotion and transmute it too, but their job is also to provide a stable platform so women can act as the vessels for this sacred process. This is men embodying the sacred masculine, so women can embody the sacred feminine to feel and express the energies that need healing and transmutation. It is not a little job. It is a great burden, but also, one of life's great gifts to be appreciated.

The problem we have though is that our society has been disconnected from this sacred and mythological way of living for several thousand years. That's some habit. And it is an embedded structure within which we live.

In Western societies, we have lost the connections to initiations and ceremonies that celebrate our movement through natural cycles of growth and development. An essential part of these cycles is experiencing the depth and even the extreme nature of our emotions. This is a descent into the world of the feminine; the dark depths of our soul and our feeling.

But to do so safely, is again, something that Western societies don't do very well. Hence, women (and men) feel unsafe when their vulnerability comes calling and asks them to experience their emotional and feeling states fully and completely.

Because of this disconnection from the sacred and archetypal parts of our human nature, both women and men have resorted to living within armoured vessels. But as much as movies and common beliefs tell us that men are the Warriors out fighting and living an armoured life of conquest and achievement, modern women are perhaps the ones who carry the most armour. And it weighs heavily, very heavily upon them, creating profound disruptions in their lives and their fields.

These restrictions upon women and men's ability to access their vulnerability safely, is described in the Heroine's Journey, as outlined by Maureen Murdoch. The first stage of the Heroine's Journey is the separation from and rejection of the feminine. This means separating yourself from aspects of the feminine, such as natural cycles, nurturing, sensitivity and compassion.

Consequences of this separation from the feminine can lead to unhealthy mother-daughter relationships, rejection of the female body, denial and avoidance of uncomfortable feelings, and an overall rejection of a sense of *being*.

The second stage is identification with the masculine. This is where many women identify as Warriors and believe they must compete in the world, just like a man, if not better than a man. It means rejecting feminine qualities, as they are seen as less-than and weak, and adopting qualities more associated with the masculine, of aggression, outwardly focussed, stoicism and competition. They are caught in the world of *doing* and looking outside of themselves for approval, satisfaction and achievement. And as with any stage on the Hero's Journey, there is always a price to pay.

This price is shown clearly in the wonderful movie, The Devil Wears Prada. In the movie, Meryl Streep's character Miranda Priestly, is the editor-in-chief of Runway, a high-fashion magazine resembling Vogue. Her subordinates are all busy and over-stretched, who are given nigh-on impossible expectations and deadlines to reach, and they live in a constant state of terror.

Miranda is the personification of perfectionism. She is an 'other-oriented perfectionist', which means she expects perfection from others and is highly judgemental and critical of their performance. It is through these qualities that she exercises power and control over her domain.

But the movie also shows the price Miranda pays for her success in the world. She has poor work/life balance, is alienated from her husband (whom she is divorcing) and her children. She is the manifestation of the idealised Superwoman; she has great fame, fortune, power and success in her field, and yet, this does not bring contentment, happiness or fulfilment.

We also see her in her vulnerability. She appears with no makeup and tells us of her awareness of the illusion of her success. We see her 'Meeting the Self' as she is humbled and aware of the price she has paid, and her complicity in abandoning her true Self.

However, Miranda doesn't change and returns to the world she has known and commanded for so long. She remains an armoured, perfect woman. And this world is to be protected. Absolutely. She demonstrates her command of power by using base-level survival energy to manipulate and control others. She will pay the price, and make sure others do too, to stay in her domain ensuring it will not be taken away from her.

Ultimately, for Miranda to be redeemed and bring forth her great wisdom from her experience in the world, she must achieve a balance between the masculine and the feminine. This is the sacred marriage. But to do so, she must let go of her attachment and need for the familiarity of the power she enjoys in her Known World. In doing so, she *would* lose everything but gain her sovereignty. This is not sovereignty by having dominion over others, which she has now, but by attaining a balance between her service to her true Self and that of the world.

This is one reason why women are defensive about being emotional and taking responsibility for that state. It is the subconscious knowing that it will lead them to lose everything; akin to 'death'. They are afraid that someone will take everything away from them.

This process of Initiation leads you into your vulnerability and exposes you to the process of breaking down your armour, your protective barriers and defences, which will ultimately lead you to your sovereignty and freedom. This is the paradox of the Journey, to gain everything, you must lose everything. And both women and men will protect themselves, to the death, from the very thing that will heal their wounding and bring them the freedom and sovereignty they so dearly want.

This is the awareness that women are protecting themselves from. It is being confronted with the reality of the façade of idealised perfection they present to themselves and the world. It confronts the reality of false expectations that can never be met. It confronts the false beliefs that need to be embraced and dispelled for women to reconcile with their Inner Self, and become the Hero that is within them.

This process takes you on the journey to confront and 'meet the Self'. You will overcome the grotesque forces 'out there', the ones that must be defended against. This monster, however, is the embodiment of the very thing lacking within you. It is your Shadow self.

In the old English tale, 'Gawain and Lady Ragnell', we see how the wounded masculine and the distorted feminine can be reconciled and healed.

King Arthur is sent on a dire quest by a fearsome and monstrous Knight to find the answer to the question: "What is it that women desire most, above all else?"

Eventually, after enduring this quest and exhausting all options, he provided the answer given to him by Lady Ragnell, a hideous, huge and grotesque woman from the forest. She told Arthur that, "What a woman desires above all else is the power of sovereignty – the right to exercise her own will."

In the story, this awareness and its implementation lead to the breaking of the spell for Lady Ragnell. After a triggering event, she appears again as her former beautiful self.

However, another condition of the spell is presented, and she asks her now-husband, the noble Gawain, to choose the shape he would like her to appear, 'the grotesque during the day and the beautiful at night, or beautiful during the day and the grotesque in their bed chamber at night'.

Gawain goes to his knees and thoughtfully answers her, that it can only be her choice to make such a decision. His answer breaks the spell completely. Lady Ragnell's sovereignty over her own will was respected, and she was free. It was a decision from the masculine to release its control over her and to respect and recognise the feminine, leading to her freedom.

(Please note that 'masculine' refers to a state of energy and being, it does not mean male. Just as 'feminine' does not mean female. Both are states of energy, awareness and being. Masculine energy is within women, as is feminine energy within men.)

The story illustrates the bringing together of the power of the 'Woman of Wisdom and Nature', and the 'Man with Heart'.

In contrast to Miranda Priestly, Lady Ragnell is not motivated by survival energies, but rather a more holistic expression of the fullness of her most true, and regal Self.

But more so, both this story and The Devil Wears Prada show us the great pressure women are under to appear a certain way in the world or be punished. They show us passionate and innate desire for sovereignty and freedom, amongst women, and the Shadow forces that go with them.

But they also show the innate power within women. In Lady Ragnell's story, this power is centred and emanates from nature. The stories show us the power women have, to protect themselves and what they are entitled to.

With Miranda Priestly however, power is demonstrated with a quiet voice of disparagement, sarcasm, manipulation and undermining others' confidence and self-esteem. This is the Shadow feminine.

And in others, this force of nature comes out in ripping and tearing and lashings out in vehement energies of abuse and blame. It is an open display of raw power to protect and defend, by getting others to pay the price.

This is the manifestation of the monster or the grotesque. In movies and in our own lives, we project this inner shadow power outward, onto some thing or someone else 'out there'. "It's him who is the danger. It's them who are terrible." But really, the greatest monster and the most grotesque being we fear, is the one we see in the mirror.

But as in all areas of the Hero/ine's Journey, there are always trials and challenges on the road to your achievement of your soul's purpose and mission. And the road to fulfilment is always through the path of vulnerability and into reconciliation with your own woundedness and greatest fears. This then brings forth a new being into the world. This is done through the very ordinary work of *taking responsibility* and being *accountable*.

This is the work that cannot happen 'out there' in the masculine world of achievement and doing, but only from the courageous inner world accessed through the feminine.

This is the gift of the Heroine's Journey.

By letting go of the armour, that weighs so heavily on so many women, a woman is then freed to engage in the much greater creative power and freedom of the sacred feminine. This is where the well-spring of creativity, wisdom, intuition and earth-power is accessed.

This is accessing the courage and power of your vulnerability. It is only by going on this journey into and through your emotions, that you uncover the great reservoir of your sovereignty, your freedom and the power of natural forces within you. It is this courage to walk into the dark places within you, and engage with them, both the monster and the grotesque, that you find the way into the light that is at your core, and then have the ability to live renewed from there.

This is why, as Marianne Williamson says in her most famous quote, "It is our light, not our darkness that most frightens us... And as we let our own light shine, we unconsciously give others permission to do the same."

This is the gift provided by the Wise Old Woman; she has seen and experienced it all. She can then provide the shelter and training for the Initiation of the new and the young. She provides the foundations for new life; the soil, the compost, the hummus that strengthens root systems from which new life grows. This is the gift of your work. It is sacred and it lives through your ordinary life. Thank you.

Oh, and my friend who started me on this journey into awareness... well, we're not friends anymore. I said something that triggered an emotional reaction... and... well, we're not friends anymore. Ahhhh... (disappointed sigh...)

Doing the Work

"If you show me a woman who can sit with a man in real vulnerability, in deep fear, and be with him in it, I will show you a woman who:

a) Has done her work, and
b) Does not derive her power from that man.

And if you show me a man who can sit with a woman in deep struggle and vulnerability and not try to fix it, but just hear her and be with her and hold space for it, I'll show you a guy who's done his work and a man who doesn't derive his power from controlling and fixing everything."

~ Brené Brown

Most people find it hard to 'step up' and take responsibility for who they are, where they are, and what they are doing in their lives. Most people prefer to rely on standard avoidance strategies of blame and distraction. But those people who do the *work*, they are the ones to cherish and hold dear.

STAGE 4: THE ABYSS

I have met some beautiful, earthy, wise women who have done the work, held this role for me. They have held me through some particularly difficult times of struggle and uncertainty in my life.

I have also met many men who have held this role for me as well. They are good men who fulfil this role in their family and work lives too. They are willing to hold themselves, often with no support and in complete isolation, whilst they experience their journey.

Doing the work means being willing to take responsibility for what is in your field and be willing to go through the process of feeling it *all the way through*. This is the work of our times. I am so grateful to know many women and men, who are willing to go on this Journey and complete the many arduous and formidable tasks of their work.

One of the lasting things I've noticed about these beautiful people is that they have stopped fighting life.

They have stopped fighting life and its natural ways and cycles. They know that life is unfair and cruel, and there is still injustice, hardship and death. But

Artist: Alexander Milov

they have stopped making this personal, and they have stopped fighting and blaming life and other people. They have learnt to accept the seasons as normal and natural, without trying to 'fix' them, but accepting what is happening *now*, and making decisions and doing the work accordingly.

It is this acceptance of the natural complexity and flow of life that makes them a beautiful force within it.

This doesn't mean they are all sunny skies, bright lights and buttercups; they are not. They are not this way, because this is not a natural state of flow. Just being 'positive' is just one end of a polarised dimension. They can be as beautiful and terrible as a force of nature. In being so, they allow others to be who they are, and where they are right now too.

The Transformation of the Warrior

I question the many memes that herald the Warrior as the most noble and superior of all archetypes.

The Warrior is a powerful archetype, no doubt. It helps you establish your identity in the world. It provides strength and capacity to create boundaries and goals for you to assert a commitment to your sense of integrity. That is, you commit to a set of values that you hold to be true.

But as with all archetypes, it has a Shadow. A Warrior in shadow moves from finding strength within, to focussing 'out there', to finding purpose in fighting, struggle and defence. In shadow, Warriors can become bullies or fundamentalists as their world view becomes narrowed into binary form, *us* or *them*. They know who they are because they know who they are against. These are signs of the Immature Warrior; the one who uses their power to aggressively assert themselves or dominate others.

But the Warrior is also a stage in your development; an important stage to help you create a healthy ego, healthy boundaries, goals to strive for and values to live by. Oftentimes people get stuck here and find it difficult to move into their next stage of growth, beyond fighting and being right and entitled. This can be difficult, as Warriors see impediments or obstacles on their journey as a call to fight or engage in war. It is worthy to note that the first part of the word 'Warrior', is war.

STAGE 4: THE ABYSS

Artist: Andriyko Podilnyk

Moving through this stage and releasing the Warrior from its prominence in your psyche may involve a profound journey into experiencing the limitations of its main driving force; will-power and determination. This often involves: failure, coming up to someone more powerful than you, experiencing limitations in your body such as sickness, injury, loss, purging and emptying. This is the emanation of the Destroyer archetype in your life.

The Destroyer is really asking the Warrior to stop endlessly focusing 'out there', to right the wrongs, fight the injustice and save the world, to in-effect stop being a spiritual, eco, social or dietary Batman or Wonder Woman.

But this stage of creative destruction is to allow the 'storm' to wreak its power inside you. That is, allow it to destroy the resistance to light and love, to break down the ego's walls, shields, weapons, and armour, to truly surrender, to be laid waste and open, to know nothing. This is death. And this is anathema to the Warrior who fears death more than anything because it symbolises failure and defeat.

This is when the other side of the Destroyer emerges: the Creator and the Mother. The Creator, the Mother or the Crone appears before you to help you, nurture you and provide succour. They show you that you need rest; deep, deep rest, and 'nothing' (no-thing) becomes your greatest friend. You do nothing. You plan nothing.

This may look like sloth and procrastination from the outside, but it is the state of emptying and allowing. It is a profound and essential stage in your growth and regeneration.

This is where a natural vacuum is created in your life. And quite naturally, as an emptying occurs in your world, the forces of nature move in, often quite subtly, to fill that space. They fill it with new life and new growth.

It is from here that a new sense of self and purpose emerges. It will appear to be very ordinary, not like the sexy Warrior, all action, certainty, and decisiveness. It will be a slow awakening or a realisation that some old burden has been released and fallen away.

And this new purpose will emerge from the earth, in respect, in compassion, in appreciation and gratitude. And from here, both your life and the Earth will be transformed and healed.

Relationships – Vessels of Transformation

Relationships are essential for your transformation and fulfillment. The most profound purpose of relationships isn't about creating and maintaining romantic love, but rather providing the vessel for your growth into your truest emanation.

Intimate relationships, because of the heightened nature of the emotions and engagement, are like crucibles as they inherently provide the heat and pressure within which humans can enhance their transformation and healing.

The stages of relationships are closely reflected in the Hero's Journey. Just as the Hero (You) goes through many trials and challenges, meeting mentors and experiencing the darkness of the Abyss, so too will a couple go through and revisit the common stages in relationships in a cyclical, not just linear manner.

These common stages of relationships are: the Merge, Doubt and Denial, Disillusionment, the Decision and Whole-hearted Love.

The Merge is akin to the first phase of the Hero's Journey, Preparation and Departure. That is, at some point you decide to leave your Known World and Cross the Threshold into the Unknown World of the relationship.

This first stage is where the couple meet and become swept up in the initial attraction, romance and overwhelming joy of each other's presence. It is a wonderful time of intoxicating emotions, sensual delights and stimulating discoveries of similarity and compatibility. Boundaries and rationality are often lost as the couple delight in their new status and revelations.

I still the remember the first time I saw the woman I would marry. It was electric. I had never experienced anything like it before. I couldn't stop smiling, which was a bit embarrassing as I was supposed to be serving her in a professional capacity. During this period of courtship, time seemed to take a long time, and there was a myriad of synchronicities we marvelled at. And our first kiss... oh, it is true that the stars shone brighter that night.

Here, goals and desires are shared, and a common future and ambitions are laid out. This is about outward thought and movement. It is engaging with the way of the masculine.

The second and third stages of relationships are akin to the second phase of the Hero's Journey, Initiation.

This movement into the masculine is what is expected from both women and men in Western societies. It is the desire for outward action, dreams and ambitions to be fulfilled, for wealth, security and adventure to be achieved.

These expectations immediately set boundaries and put pressure upon a relationship. Income goals and career expectations are set, as are social and familial interactions. Often though, these expectations are unstated and unconsciously held. There are expectations of what each partner should do and should bring to the relationship. There are expectations of what a man should do, what he should provide and how he should behave.

Expectations for women, however, have changed significantly over the recent decades. A woman is now not expected to be passive in a relationship (unless she wants to) as she was in the 1950s and before; now she has expectations for career and personal expression and to be supported in doing it. Women are now much more power-centres within relationships and in society, and there are expectations and resources supporting this reality.

So, as the couple Crosses the Threshold into the new world of the relationship, they encounter Doubt and Denial. This is where the couple begin to realise that their ideal partner, 'twin flame', or 'soul-mate', is actually a separate human being with differences and issues. They wake up out of their infatuation and find that their partner's quirkiness is more like insecurity, their reliability is rigidity, stability is boring and that being 'goal-oriented' can be obsessive and selfish.

Often, the couple tries to mould their partner into a reflection of themselves. They want their partner to change to support their sense of identity. The focus is outward in order to bring satisfaction inward, hence, the way of the masculine.

But during this stage, misunderstandings and miscommunications ensue as expectations are not met, bringing on friction and uncertainty. This can be disconcerting as the once-harmonious connection is led into a new world of competing agendas and worldviews. Personal wounds can be triggered, leading to defensiveness, distrust and power struggles.

This is where the profound nature of relationships begins. Heat and pressure begin to build up in the crucible that will eventually lead to breakdown and transformation.

Issues surrounding identity emerge such as habits, beliefs, values and perceptions, which are now questioned, doubted or attacked. The certainty of this previous worldview is now defended as an act of survival.

The underlying belief and identity structures are now exposed. Hence arguments, power struggles and the undermining and sabotaging of each other grow in frequency and intensity. Issues can be brought up, but as the underlying structure of insecurity and woundedness are not understood or acknowledged, the relationship will return to the same old patterns. This is when couples either look for healthier ways to disagree and communicate, or they begin the process of breaking up.

I gained so much from my marriage. I learnt about the complexities within an individual and how can rule thinking and behaviour. I saw how childhood issues show up and are projected outward onto your partner. I experienced how denial is a foundational survival mechanism, and the devastation that my wife didn't share my desire for a successful marriage.

The third stage in the relationship is Disillusionment. This is aligned with the fourth stage of the Hero's Journey, the Abyss. This is where it can seem that the relationship is a war zone or a barren landscape. There is no love and no joy. There is routine, disinterest and indifference or even resentment, disdain and hostility. There may be ongoing power struggles and resistance to healthy communication. Long-term issues that could have been uncovered and dealt with are actively bypassed, defended vigorously or turned into battles. This outward seeking of resolution through blame, control or manipulation is the expression of the immature masculine and demonstrates how energy follows the path of least resistance. It shows how patterns will continue, until something comes along to break them. This is the purpose of the crucible and the Abyss.

Depression and despair can be keenly felt at this time, as can the desire for escapism and wishing for a life beyond the current reality. Accordingly, some people seek consolation and refuge by having affairs, working too much, creating a shadow-life, or finding ways to survive by actively disconnecting and disengaging from their partner and family life.

But again, the crucible that is the relationship is part of your Hero's Journey. It is calling you to go to your depths, to uncover and heal your wounds and to step into your greatest gifts. This fall inward and downward, into your woundedness, despair and darkness, is the way of the sacred feminine. It is the way to your healing, redemption and enlightenment. And because it is painful, difficult and even terrifying, most people don't go there. This is why most first marriages so often fail.

It is here that the greatest heat and pressure is brought to bear. You are being Initiated. It is the way of your soul and your Hero's Journey.

During this stage, betrayals can be uncovered. Deep and long-held childhood pains, wounds and untrue beliefs that have been denied or bypassed can be brought to light. This leads inevitably into the Abyss: the place of darkness, despair and death.

Here, the couple may either slowly or brutally break apart. They may disengage and reaffirm their commitment to their previous identity and goals, or they may walk the path of discovery and faith, revealing a new structure for themselves.

For me, I felt deeply betrayed by my ex-wife's determination to end our marriage. It was like watching a kid at the beach kicking down a sandcastle which they had built together with someone else. There was such glee and sense of power at seeing our creation being actively destroyed.

From here, the couple move into the fourth stage, Decision, which is aligned with the third phase of the Hero's Journey, the Return.

In this stage the couple decide to either leave, stay and make peace with a miserable situation, or reconcile and grow into a new relationship and structure.

To stay means doing the Work. The Work means Crossing a Threshold and taking responsibility for your role in creating and maintaining the relationship. This involves learning new skills in listening and communicating, and dealing with difficult and sensitive issues. This too, is accessing the way of the feminine. It is the journey into wisdom and maturity. This is the path of the courageous vulnerable.

As I found out so painfully, when couples have different ways of dealing with issues, it makes it unlikely their relationship will survive. If one wants to do the Work and the other doesn't, then the relationship will end. Some prefer to maintain old patterns; the patterns that have kept them safe all their lives.

And finally, you reach the fifth stage in your relationship, Wholehearted Love. This is part of the final stage of the Hero's Journey. This is where the richness of the relationship is found. The heat and pressure that has been experienced in this crucible, has brought forth new beings into a new structure. There is now mutual respect and appreciation for each other and the relationship. Intimacy is regenerated and communication is enhanced as the couple experience true individuation, interdependence, self-discovery and the nourishment of acceptance and recognition.

Both the Hero and the Heroine's Journey show us pathways to discover and then uncover our inherent gifts and talents, and often the way we do that is through struggle and pain. Relationships are part of this great process of transformation. They provide both the agony and the ecstasy of being in communion with ourselves, our partner and the community, and also the opportunity to discover our soul's purpose through them all.

Grandiosity and Awakening

Breakdowns serve the purpose of 'breaking down' old structures of thought, perception, patterns and belief. They are essential for your development and fulfilment.

In terms of the Hero's Journey, these breakdowns are symbolic of the Abyss or Death stage. It is the most profound stage where the limitations of the old ways are seen and experienced.

Breakdowns come in the form of devastations, annihilations, abandonment, illness and pressure. They show you in graphic terms, that you cannot

*"Sometimes people say, "What's the secret of
a long marriage?""*
"Well... you don't get divorced."

**Olivia Harrison,
married to George Harrison for 23 years.**

control the world, other people, or outcomes anymore. You may lose everything. Everything. And yes, I know, *it's hard. Really hard.*

Many people experience occasions of divine intervention, spiritual awakening, kundalini rising, or visions during these intense times. It is an incredibly powerful, often wrenching, visceral experience. During this time, you often gain grand visions of your true purpose and a new life.

This is where many people often get caught up in wanting to become yogis or shamans, healers, spiritual teachers or therapists. The Lover and the Seeker archetypes become active in your life as you search out the perfect forum for your new skills, visions and dreams.

You may see the darkness and unfairness in the world and join groups or 'tribes' or other like-minded 'activists', to fight the problems and create the *new world* of your visions.

This process occurred for boxer George Foreman after he lost the 1974 heavyweight title fight to Muhammad Ali in Zaire. After the loss, Foreman went through a devastating period of depression and decline. From this he emerged, after being 'born again', as a Christian preacher and minister.

When possessed by grandiosity, a false self can take over. This can show up when you change your name to reflect your new exotic and 'spiritual' persona. You may adopt a new lifestyle, live in an ideal location, get a new job and relationships to reflect this new structure in your life. This grandiose person may become very impatient and judgemental towards others who are not pursuing the same vision and dreams you are.

The shadow side of grandiosity though can lead people into becoming dissociated from reality. They can become self-absorbed, narcissistic and totally ungrounded in their expectations of themselves, others and the world around them. They believe they know everything and see everything with complete clarity. They may believe their visions are derived from divine powers or higher spirits. They can become hyper-sensitive, defensive, reactive and judgemental.

Grandiosity appears when you lose your boundaries with God/Source or Spirit. You believe you really are *the* Spirit. You really are, All That Is and therefore you know, *all* that there is to know.

The most dangerous part is when you don't know you are embodying grandiosity. Often this is because you haven't created healthy boundaries in your childhood or elsewhere. You don't know who 'you' are, and how you are differentiated from others. You haven't created a healthy ego structure to enable you to understand and appreciate 'I' and 'me'.

Grandiosity can then work in harmony with your denial of deeply-held woundedness to become totally focussed on issues 'out there', and become even more self-absorbed and ungrounded. Consequently, your healing, as well as your growth, is avoided and postponed.

So, when you do have these awakening crises, you may become possessed by your predominant archetype or shadow. Hence you may become a *super* Warrior, or *super* Healer, or a *super* Mystic or Shaman.

But through the process of your journey, there must be a balance. So just as the grandiose takes you up, out and away, the power of the Journey and your Soul brings you down and back to earth, often through humiliation, loss and devastation. You are humbled. The Destroyer archetype ensures you don't get too far away from earth.

You experience *all* of All That Is. It is like an energetic, emotional and mental tsunami coming through you, overwhelming you and completely devastating all previous structures and certainties within you.

This is when you really need grounded friends and support. You need therapies that help ground and integrate these new energies, and allow the old ways to be honoured, grieved for, and released.

This is when the truly *new* being emerges, humble and tentative at first. This is when the Creator archetype shows up in your life, to help sow the seeds of your new beginning. This process can then either cripple you, as you get overwhelmed by the fathomless nature of the transformation or be profoundly healed and engaged in the metamorphosis.

For George Foreman, now in his 70s, this process appears to have helped him emerge from his devastation with a greater appreciation of himself, his life's journey (including his defeats, especially at the hands of Ali), and the world around him. His journey was to achieve grandiose success (champion of the world), be defeated and devastated, be 'born again', and go on a grandiose evangelical crusade to save the world, then to emerge into a place of greater trust and love for himself and others.

Ahhhh... the Journey. Grandiosity and devastation, it's all part of the Hero's Journey. And by going through it, you are serving a greater purpose than you may know at the time.

Questions and Exercises:

1. When, where and how has 'The Abyss' showed up in your life.
   - Name three occasions when you know you experienced an Abyss in your life.
   - What were the gifts and the pressures the Abyss brought to you?
   - What archetypes did Abyss bring up for you? Eg: the Hero, the Victim, the Healer, the Magical Child, the Mentor, the Rescuer, the Vampire, the Saboteur, etc?
   - What 'triggered' the Abyss? What do you think were the underlying causes of your movement into the Abyss?
2. Looking back, what three things do you think you were supposed to learn from the Abyss?
3. How did you respond to the various trials and challenges you were presented during the Abyss? Name two that you know you responded well to, and two that you know you didn't respond well.
4. What pressures were upon you to make decisions during the Abyss?
   - How did you make your decisions?
5. Name three things from this part of the book that moved you or struck you as important.
6. Creative expression - drawing: Take some time to find a quiet space. Breathe deeply and relax your body. Feel the breath go all the way through your body, and clear your mind. With paper, coloured pencils or crayons in front of you, ask yourself clearly, "Show me what is important for me to know from this part of the book."

   Then, with your non-dominant hand, choose a pencil or crayon, and start drawing. It doesn't matter what it looks like, just create. Change hands when your body tells you. Repeat.

Stage 5: Rebirth and Transformation

Having faced the terrors from journeying into the darkest spaces and enduring the darkest of times, the Hero (You) survives and is transformed.

Emerging exhausted and renewed, you continue on your way on the Ascent, to acquire new skills and bring forth your gifts and talents into the world.

You engage with your community in new and different ways. You give thanks for where and who you have been, and you atone for all whom you have hurt and wounded on your journey, including yourself.

The rewards received are things like renewed physical health and well-being, romantic love, spiritual expansion and enhancement and career advancement and material wealth. And often, the initial quest or dream you pursued becomes secondary as a result of your personal and spiritual transformation.

Now renewed, you take greater satisfaction in being of service to others and the community.

Our Greatest Mission and Purpose

Perhaps our greatest mission, purpose, and achievement, is to break old patterns: old untrue beliefs, generational or inter-generational patterns of abuse and old karmic ways. This is the breaking of the old structure that ruled your life and the outcomes you achieved.

Your journey has served you to get you to where you are now; to the place where you can now step into your truest expression of your Self – that of a being of love and power, in service to the betterment of all.

By doing so, you bring all things back into balance, and back into harmony. This is truly a blessed and successful, soul-full life.

And you only know this, after you have done it.

The Dance of Emergence

> *"Enlightenment is nothing more than the complete absence of resistance to what is. End of story."*
>
> **- Adyashanti, Emptiness Dancing**

There is a mystery in transformation. There is a cloud that is moved through. It is a cloud of portent, filled with uncertainty, doubt and apprehension.

The heart leads, then the body, and the head is the last to move through.

The body is the vehicle that allows the transcendence of the soul, up from the earth, both exultant and excruciating in its experience.

It is the humbling of the spirit that is essential for our emergence. The spirit lives in the exultant space of purity, perfection and elevated states of love and bliss.

As we transform, as we move into the cloud of portent, we begin, alone, in nature. We begin the dance of destruction and resurrection. We begin, grounded, attuned to nature and alive in faith and hope.

But the head is the last to move. It loves being *right* and being in the familiar. Supported by the spirit to seek higher truths, the head conceptualises, justifies and denies the movement to humbling.

Artist: Seonjun Kang

But the heart leads and the body moves through, despite its resistance to past wounds and fears.

And the head, with all of its theories and concepts, righteousness and entitlement, is always the last to do so.

There is an excruciating exaltation in birthing a new way, a new life and new being.

And then, as the body rejoices, relaxes and enjoys each new breath, there is laughter. There is joy.

And a new life begins.

The Call of the Crone and Earth-Based Wisdom

The Crone accesses earth and nature wisdom which has not been valued highly for a long time. The Crone and the Wise Old Man are both aligned with Earth and nature wisdom. They access ancient lore, myths and archetypes which are all part of our greater human consciousness and energy fields. This is what we have collectively been shut-off from for several hundred, if not, a thousand years or more.

The rise of the 'scientific' mind has meant that limitations of logic and rationality have ruled how people define and therefore, perceive and experience the world. These limitations are playing themselves out 'loudly' right now, amongst both the keepers of the status quo, and those who see themselves as the great 'Liberators' and 'Revolutionaries' of our times. They are expressing themselves within an oscillating structure of reaction and response. But a new way is called for right now. And it is rising.

The Crone, the Forest Hermit, the Earth Sage, the Wise Fool and the Alchemist are all archetypes that are calling us right now.

We are being called to release, and allow to die, those previous perceptions, ruled by the mind and the ego (based in 3D and 4D) and their consequent identities.

It is time to acknowledge the call of the earth and our soul, and immerse ourselves in its timelessness and the power and wisdom that comes from that. And then... follow that call. Act upon it. Don't 'trust' that things will be ok before you act, just Know. That Knowing is your calling.

It is not a calling into passiveness or aggressiveness, but into acceptance of who you truly are, what you truly want (your Vision aligned with your true nature), and where you are right now.

And it is as easy and as difficult as that.

Sing to the Night

"Sing to the night", the desert said. "Sing to the night, and grace us with your open heart."

And the desert and the night rejoiced as she shared her open heart with the world.

She was tired, hungry and thirsty. She had walked and walked through the night, away from her home, away from the hurt and the betrayal. Her inner voice had called her, propelled her and directed her on her way, and she trusted her inner voice. She listened, and so she began.

She began with an inward movement, unsure of what to do. Her pain called up within her saying, "No! No! Don't! Do not open yourself! Protect yourself!"

But she trusted the night, the desert and the moon, and she continued.

Slowly her pain felt comforted by her body. Her body welcomed the pain and said, "Come through me and you will be transformed. Let me release you."

And so, her pain moved through her body. Like a wave, it swelled and grew, and then frothed and hurled.

At times excruciating; feeling the betrayal, the heartache, the distrust and the abandonment. All these feelings welled up, coming forth, and asking to break within her.

She cried out to the moon for help and asked the desert to swallow her up. "How could they do that to me?!" she cried and fell to her knees.

A deep mournful cry came up from her body, up from the desert and up to the moon. It carried all her hurt, all her powerlessness, all her rage and all her despair. The yearning for love and comfort swept through and out of her, and was eventually washed away.

She was exhausted, and completely empty now. Completely empty. She collapsed onto the ground.

And as she got up, slowly and with strain, she heard the moon say, "Thank you. Thank you. You have transformed your pain, and you have changed the world. You are empty now. Rest."

STAGE 5: REBIRTH AND TRANSFORMATION

Artist: Carla Vega

And the desert said, "Thank you. Rest now. You will be filled again soon enough."

And she rested. She sat, not knowing what would come next, but just allowing the wind to blow and the sky to open unto the new day.

And as the sun rose above the horizon, she stood slowly and smiled. "Yes," she said. "Yes. I will open my heart. I will open my heart to the world." And she sighed and smiled as tears welled up. "Yes, I will open my heart to the world."

She looked down and laughed. She turned behind her and recognised the path that had brought her to this place and gave thanks. "Thank you to you all", she said, putting her hands to her heart in prayer.

She stood up, faced the morning sun, opened her heart, and sang. She sang for the world. She sang for her pain. She sang in gratitude, and she sang in relief. She sang for her renewal. She was coming home.

And the moon and the desert smiled.

Gratitude and Appreciation

I appreciate the courage of a soul to embody into this world.

And this is a harsh world, no doubt.

And to embody at this time of profound change and disruption, *and* to be the ones who are choosing to do the Work of transformation and transmutation... Wow!

That is true courage personified, as ordinary as it may seem.

It's where I appreciate the courage of those who literally choose to 'show up' in courses and programs and groups that challenge people to change and move through the issues that come up.

They choose to go on the Journey into the dark places and face the Shadow-self, their fears and wounds, and find the ways to reconciliation. Eventually, their Journey leads them to self-appreciation and self-love. This is the place of new beginnings.

These things truly change the world and allow others to move into their capacity to do the same.

This is the movement into engaging with your Soul and your grand purpose. It's not about achieving the goals that you 'think' are your purpose, like 'saving the world', 'changing everybody else', having romantic relationships, etc. It's actually much bigger and more ordinary than that.

This moment of awareness can happen in the midst of a **'loud'** classroom of twenty-five grade 2s, or in the stillness of the morning with a cuppa tea, or watching a couple at the cafe dealing with their two little ones. It takes just a moment. A moment of appreciation just to stop and become aware of who and what is around you.

There is so much beauty, so much heart and goodwill all around you. In that moment of awareness, you experience the power and expansion that comes from appreciation and gratitude. This is grace.

So, I honour you and bow to you as a courageous soul who is engaging fully in this Journey. Thank you.

Giving Up and Surrendering Are Not the Same

"Giving up is refusing to participate in your experience.
Surrender is ending your fight against your experiences,
even if your experiences continue fighting you.

In surrender, you are not giving up, but giving up your fight against
the discomfort of outcome and circumstance."

Matt Kahn, Spiritual Teacher

Caring and feeling are some of the most courageous things you can do in your life. Shutting down and flipping off, blaming others and staying in your Victimhood can provide short-term relief. Although, some people have made this sort of bypassing and avoidance a central part of their lives.

As you learn to love yourself first, as you practice this more and more, you realise that this is one of the greatest gifts and practices you can bring to the world.

Yes, it's not sexy like going on a protest march, but it is profound, simple and life-changing. Caring and feeling is how you show you have survived the heartaches, betrayals and traumas of your life. It is not a weakness. You are not losing anything. You are demonstrating the courage to engage fully with **all** of life, even in its most raw and painful places. This is engaging with the grace and power of the divine feminine in your life.

The Three Most Difficult Things

Someone once said, "The three most difficult things for a human being are not physical feats or intellectual achievements. They are, first, returning love for hate; second, including the excluded; and third, admitting that you are wrong."

**Anthony De Mello, from Awareness –
The Perils and Opportunities of Reality**

STAGE 5: REBIRTH AND TRANSFORMATION

As you emerge, refreshed and renewed, cleansed and clear from this exercise, it feels like you have emerged from a swim in the ocean or a lake. There is a tingly aliveness you feel all the way through your body. Your senses become heightened and clear. You can then share this new awareness and sensation with the world, bringing joy and comfort to others.

As part of my life's journey, I experienced a time where I had to give up my dreams and goals. All of them. It was completely dispiriting, and I knew this was the only choice I had left. I chose to be here now, listen to my body, attend to my health, and live one day at a time, one moment at a time and put one foot in front of the other. I had a faithful knowing that I would be guided to where I was supposed to be. It was a heart-wrenching, body-sapping period of facing the truth of what the Universe was telling me. I had to surrender and let it all go.

For a long time later, I still didn't have much money, a car, a relationship, or a definite idea about my future. But I did have a sense of peace and ease which grew over time. I also knew, after a long struggle, that I had been living my life's purpose, even when it was dark and grim. I learnt to appreciate my journey through that dark forest and barren landscape, as actually serving a greater purpose than what I knew at the time.

Birthing My True Self

Slowly
Emerging
Out from the old,
The mud,
The heartache,
Powerlessness and fatigue,
I am birthing.
Birthed
Out of humility,
Out of pain,
Out of renouncing
All that was before,
Into freedom, and
Into light.
Into the light
I serve

And shine.
My True Self.
I am humbled, and
Grateful.
Thank you.
Thank you for your journey.
You have led me,
To where I need to be.
Reconciled and
Renewed.
Anew
All that I AM.
Here,
And now.
I am grateful.
And always,
I am loving.

The Past Really Did Happen

The past really did happen. The memories of it are stored in your cells, in your DNA and your energy field. Your past is part of you. It can show up in your life in your talents, abilities and gifts, like musical ability, creativity and intelligence. Or it can show up in your health and behaviour, such as allergies, depression, addiction, avoidance patterns, or in motivation, strength and compassion.

Positive thinking doesn't clear or change anything in this part of you. It may just lead you into years of denial. But, if you really want to clear the past from your system, then you must *face* it and deal with it. You must face the uncomfortable feelings, the senses, the memories, and the dreams; all of it. You must enter the Abyss. These emotions and memories can only be cleared once you have recognised them and acknowledged them; thereby giving them the respect that is their due.

It **is** uncomfortable for sure. But it is the only way that you can clear the past from your energy field. You must engage with it.

This means taking responsibility and being accountable for who you are, what you are doing and what you have done. This means paying attention to what is going on in your body and your broader energy field.

This also means following the process that will inevitably lead to your humbling; recognising that you don't know everything, you can't do everything, you don't get everything *right*, and you can't control everybody and everything 'out there'.

For some people, completing this clearing process is their life's work. This is their Soul's purpose in this lifetime: to clear their field so others do not have to experience the pain and torment of the past's energetic memories. Hence, they may experience great ill health, injustice, or hardship in many forms. Their work in this lifetime may be to experience these conditions so they can then be transmuted and transcended.

I have the utmost respect for those who go through such a journey. Seeking assistance through a good counsellor, healer or therapist can help get in touch with these unconscious and shunned parts of yourself. I have had many profound sessions with counsellors and healers over the years. They have helped me clear and reconcile with long-held tendencies to self-sabotage and self-blame.

By going through this work of clearing and healing and getting out of denial, you bring yourself more fully, truly and compassionately into the world. This **is** bringing peace to the world because you are bringing peace, harmony and reconciliation to yourself and within yourself, first. You then *walk as peace* in the world, rather than just talking it, thinking it, or lecturing others about it.

Life isn't fair. It's not supposed to be and attending to your journey is the best thing you can do to change the world into the glorious place it will inevitably become. We are the ones the world has been waiting for.

Self-Blame Is One of The Cancers of Your Life

Self-blame is one of the cancers of your life. Believing that you are *the* cause of *all* that happens to you in your life, is a delusion.

We are walking through life doing the best we can, and often we adopt belief systems and behaviour patterns to protect us from a world that we experience as unsafe. I know I did.

Often, most often, these beliefs are false. Things like: 'I'm dumb', 'I'm not good enough', 'It was because of me', 'I'm not lovable', 'I must fulfil family expectations', are common examples. These beliefs are not true; but you believe them. You truly believe them, and paradoxically, you spend a lot of time and energy denying that you believe them. You thereby create a powerful defence system against your freedom and salvation.

You cannot walk around with these false beliefs openly, so you construct a powerful system of denial enabling you to survive in the world. This becomes the driving force for your life. Many people have been driven to great success fuelled by their denial of their basic, untrue beliefs about themselves and their purpose.

I have seen many people move into disconnection of how they feel, or play 'good', by doing what they 'should', as they play out this pattern. The pattern had to be played out so that it can end, and this was the choice of your soul.

By completing this process and enduring the hardship and pain of disconnection and numbing, you experience the uncovering of your untrue beliefs. By doing so, you undergo a most arduous initiation into finding and experiencing your true value and character; you uncover your true Self.

There are many men and women who courageously walk their own soul's path, as difficult as it is. It is often a path of engaging and healing personal wounds to clear the way for others. They have the courage to experience some of the lowest and darkest of moments like intense numbness, or an incessant feeling of pain, disappointment, worthlessness and humiliation. And they make it through.

After that, they must go through the grief cycle as they let go of that, now completed, part of their life. They engage with the different stages of the grief cycle, from anger and denial, to acceptance and finally, making meaning. They find meaning and value in going through this whole immense journey.

I don't believe that life is like a Nike ad, *Just do it!* Life is far more complex, more deeply challenging than a simplistic slogan. It is about completing your soul contracts, as painful and arduous as that is, and moving into ease, meaning and maturity.

I am grateful to those people around me that have helped me into this understanding, by showing me what courage and nobility really look like. We are truly surrounded by ordinary heroes.

"So, the last will be first and the first last…" Matthew, 19:29-30

I can feel a life coming to an end. A life that has seen me be one of "the *last*" for a long, long time. That is, for a long time I had limited resources, no job, no career, no relationships, poor health and low energy. I felt I had no power and no path to enable me to achieve my goals, my dreams and my potential. And this is finally coming to an end.

And for others, their paths have seen them achieve wealth and status, relationship success, establish families and create long-term paths to learning and achievement. Some have become masters in their fields, skills and professions.

But the world is changing. We are in a time of profound disruption and upheaval. Truth is 'fake', and 'fake' is truth. This is a time when the societal order is being challenged, upset and overturned.

This is also happening on an energetic level, where people's lives are being disrupted as more and more people are listening to their awakening Self and take direction from within. It's time to let go and move on from old identities, paradigms and structures. Old energetic structures of thought and belief are being transmuted from your system, and a new pattern, a new structure of energy and vibration is being installed and integrated.

Forgiveness is a Key to Freedom

Forgiveness is truly one of the greatest keys to freedom.
Forgiving and releasing all those 'out there' who
have hurt and betrayed you.
And finally, the greatest gift of all, forgiving and releasing yourself.
Always the hardest and last thing you do.
Peace

We are being directed by the Universe to 'become as little children' (Matthew, 18:3). That is, to allow ourselves to not know what that will happen but be present with what *is* happening at this moment. We are being asked to experience life with awe and wonder, with openness and courage (the way of the Innocent or Child archetypes), rather than through fear, calculation and control.

The way of the new is to allow yourself to become like a child. Allow yourself to walk in innocence, where everything is a completely new discovery. You are filled with awe and acceptance of what is in your world, and *know* you are safe.

I have noticed this is very difficult for many who are highly skilled in their fields, particularly in personal growth and healing work, as well as those who identify strongly with the Warrior and Healer archetypes.

It's hard to let go and leave behind your successes, your knowledge, and even your fights and wounds. By holding onto them, you believe you can prove how right you are, and justify the amount of time and money you've spent in acquiring this knowledge and these skills. But to leave it behind and trust the path that emerges is, no doubt, particularly challenging and an act of trust and faith.

It is time to put down your swords and shields and armour, and truly open yourself in trust, acceptance and love. It *is* safe now.

It is a time where the sacred feminine is awakening in your life after being cocooned underground for a long time. This time of cocooning feeds the soul and allows for deep roots to grow and establish themselves. It is a time where the sacred fire awakens within and warms the body, whilst outside the season has just turned; it may still be harsh, cold and barren but the new shoots are emerging from below, from the earth.

Overseeing this change for you, are your archetypal guides and spirit friends. In the Hero's Journey, this character is often a Crone or a Merlin-type, Gandalf character from the forest or the earth. They are normally an older woman or man who knows the seasons of life, the Earth and the soul. They are awaiting your awakening. They are overseeing your rebirth into the world. They are ready to serve, protect and mentor you as the new shoots in your life arise. They usher you on your path to wisdom, sovereignty and service. They let you know from within, that you are safe and your future is assured.

STAGE 5: REBIRTH AND TRANSFORMATION

Artist: Walkmaz

Be the Vessel of Transformation

You show me, through your open and raw vulnerability, that we humans, so ordinary and courageous that we are, are truly the vessels of transformation and transmutation.

It is through feeling that which is in our fields, as painful as it is, that we enable the transformation and the healing of the world.

Be the vessel of transformation. Become empty. There is purpose in being empty. An empty vessel is no less purposeful than a full one. It is filled with potential and awaiting its call to service.

There are many containers that are filled with outdated and unused stuff. They are often mouldy and smelly, or so disused that they are stuck hard, so much so that they cannot be opened without breaking them. These structures cannot perform at all.

Be the empty vessel. Release all that oldy, mouldy, unsafe and unused material. Open yourself, clear it out and get rid of it. Be empty and allow yourself to wait. There is purpose in this state.

This is how you create the change you want to see in the world, by going through this raw and vulnerable process of emptying and transformation.

Thank you for being the alchemist's vessel and going on the journey to transform and transmute the heavy and leaden energies within your field, into living gold.

Questions and Exercises:

1. Give some thought as to when, where and how you experienced a 'Rebirth and Transformation' in your life.
   - Name two occasions when you know you experienced a Rebirth.
   - What were the gifts and the pressures the Rebirth brought to you?
   - What 'triggered' your Transformation?
   - What archetypes did the Rebirth bring up for you? Eg: the Hero, the Martyr, the Healer, the Magical Child, the Hermit, the Rescuer, the Teacher, the Warrior etc?
2. Looking back, what three things do you think you were supposed to learn from the Transformation process?
3. How did you respond to the various trials and challenges you were presented during your Rebirth stage? Name two that you know you responded well to, and two that you know you didn't respond well.
4. What pressures were upon you to make decisions during your Rebirth?
   - How did you make your decisions?
   - Did you respond with grandiosity or with humility and clarity?
5. Name at least three gifts you gained from experiencing this Rebirth and Transformation process.
6. Name three things from this part of the book that moved you or struck you as important.
7. Creative expression - drawing: Take some time to find a quiet space. Breathe deeply and relax your body. Feel the breath go all the way through your body, and clear your mind. With paper, coloured pencils or crayons in front of you, ask yourself clearly, "Show me what is important for me to know from this part of the book."

   Then, with your non-dominant hand, choose a pencil or crayon, and start drawing. It doesn't matter what it looks like, just create. Change hands when your body tells you. Repeat.

Phase 3:
The Return

The Return is the final phase in the Hero's Journey. It is a phase of great consequence as you are consciously stepping away from your previous life of Initiation through struggle, and into a new and more humble and abundant way of life.

It is a phase where you have cleared your debts and released your burdens of guilt and grief and shame, and healed your long-held wounds and false beliefs. You have moved through your time of humbling and your atonement for the hurts you have experienced or done to others.

To cross the threshold into this new way of living will also bring up fears, doubts and uncertainties. But this is because you are expanding and growing into a whole new way of being in the world. Doing so is a step into freedom by uncovering more of the depth of your joy and hope and love, and having the confidence to express it in the world.

Stage 6:
The Road Back - Rewards and Gifts

Even though You (the Hero) has been through an arduous journey that has resulted in death and rebirth, the adventure isn't over yet. Now you must return to the world from which you came as your new Self, bringing your gifts and talents.

New trials and challenges lie ahead in the form of temptations, roadblocks, and inner demons. You must deal with whatever issues are left unresolved through this stage of the journey.

This means you re-examine your morals and values, and the way you have lived your life. You are aware of the power of your shadow and how that has lived through you in your life. You Atone for the harm you have done to others, and to your Self. And you emerge with greater appreciation, wisdom and love for your Self and the world.

When beginning a new life,
you don't need to sprint to the start line

The Tyranny of the Big Life Purpose

My soul's purpose is Big. I know that for sure. But the steps to get there are small and are applied, a little bit at a time, in my ordinary life.

There's nothing wrong with that. That's how big things get created; a little bit at a time, from the ground up.

It took a long time for me to recognise and accept that. It was a long and painful and frustrating process.

Often you don't realise what the purpose of an event, a job, or a relationship is until a long time later. That's the hard part. You are living and fulfilling your life's purpose without knowing that you are doing it at the time.

For years I felt great pressure to achieve my goals, missions, visions and purpose. I went through an arduous period of ill-health, depression, poverty and failure, that lasted over ten years, without seemingly achieving any of them. Now I know, I was fulfilling my life's purpose by going through that time of hardship, even though I didn't know it at the time.

The purpose was for me to become the catalyst for healing and clearing generational, intergenerational, and past-life issues. The suffering I experienced was there for me to feel, transmute and thereby heal all that was in my field.

I realised afterwards, that by living my ordinary life, I was living my life's purpose. My purpose is not separate from me at all.

I realised my soul knows my purpose. My soul knows my soul's purpose better than I do.

My soul's job is to lead me into the circumstances and connect me with the people I need to enable me to achieve this purpose. This could look like a successful business and a beautiful relationship, or it could be achieved in a noisy chaotic classroom where I have spent most of my working life.

My job is to take the small steps that are open to me at the time to live out my big purpose.

These were things like applying kindness, honesty, humility, compassion, active listening, respect, gratitude and trust in my life.

In my teaching work, I applied these qualities diligently over time. These are all big values delivered to little kids, making huge differences in short periods, and accumulated over longer spaces of time, to bring profound change.

I can also apply these values in whatever I do, from washing the dishes to dealing with chaotic grade 2s, to rude and belligerent year 8s. These values and virtues are often very challenging to apply. And they are all the little steps in achieving my grand purpose.

And it is achieved over time through my journey in my ordinary life. I know that fulfilling my purpose is not a destination, but attending to and implementing small things in my ordinary life. And I breathe easily knowing that I have done my part.

Confidence is Freedom - Wisdom from a Child

"This course has changed my life", said the boy enthusiastically. "I just didn't know before that confidence means you can feel free. I always thought it meant you were supposed to be powerful. But for the first time in my life, I feel free!"

As said by a grade five student after completing a course in public speaking. He felt free. He felt unfettered by his previous doubts, fears and experience about his ability to speak publicly. He experienced himself as confident and at ease with himself - free, with no need to dominate or be forceful over others. He made the distinction between feeling *free* and feeling *powerful*.

He thought that being confident meant you had to be *powerful* in the world. That is, power over others or the power to control things in the world. But he found that this was not what confidence was to him. After completing the eight-week course, where the students must first create and then give a speech in front of their peers and parents, he found that he gained a greater sense of ease within himself.

This confidence and freedom were embodied on their graduation night, where the students performed their speeches. It is an incredibly moving event, as the new skills the students have practised are seen and celebrated by the audience of family and peers.

One of the greatest gifts you get as a teacher is seeing the transformation of a student over time. You see them demonstrate this transformation with skills and abilities they have learnt, which just a short time ago, they thought they could never do. I witnessed the demonstration of these speaking skills with confidence, engagement, humour and a willingness to take risks, right in front of me. It is both inspiring and humbling to facilitate such an event.

All students; extroverted and introverted, on the autistic spectrum, learning difficulties, quiet ones, loud ones, one with a broken foot, another with a sore throat, and even one with chickenpox, got up and performed their speeches on the night.

They demonstrated poise, confidence, inspiration, courage, ability to deal with mistakes and stumbles, humour, insight, quirkiness, perseverance and a strong celebration of bringing forth their unique selves.

One boy's mother was so moved by his performance that she was in tears at the end of the night saying, "He is the 'quiet one'". He is the one who says little in class and doesn't participate in activities and isn't very good in games. Well, on that night, Anthony wasn't like that, he demonstrated his true self.

Anthony gets up, and with quirky confidence, delivers his speech. He uses various gestures throughout, sweeping us this way and that way through his various points. He used his vocal range, going quiet and leaning forward, and then loudly calling forth his next point, demonstrating humour and insight.

Anthony had the opportunity to show this side of himself, unleashed from his fears and expectations. This was a boy embodying a sense of freedom, and in this demonstration, Anthony found his confidence, and his power.

Another boy, Liam, who has significant literacy issues, gets up and performs his 'Lantern Breaths' (the breathing exercise at the heart of the Yellow Lantern public speaking program). Liam stands strongly in front of the assembled parents and students. He takes a deep breath in and begins his speech. Half-way through, his voice cracks as he hits that point of 'I can't'. I move closer to him to assist him at this moment. I whisper "breathe..." He followed the procedure he had practised before. He stops, stands strongly, takes a deep breath in, his chest moves up and down, his voice, posture and stance are all strong now. Liam continues. This happened one more time.

Liam's voice cracked again. He stopped, and he knew the routine to get himself back on track. I stood close by and just made a loud in-breath sound. He stood strongly and deliberately and breathed in deeply. His chest moved up and allowed the breath to slowly come down into his body, and he continued. Liam spoke slowly and deliberately, emphasising the words he had highlighted. He finished his final line and said, "thank you" to the crowd, who then ALL spontaneously erupted in huge applause. "Yaaaaa!", they exclaimed with delight, pride, and relief.

Everyone was so pleased, not just that he made it through, but that he made it through with strength and self-assurance, demonstrating all that he had learnt. He actively applied the method taught to him, to speak fully and completely. He did it. He demonstrated what freedom looks like, and everyone in that room was affected by that inspirational act.

I too was demonstrably affected by that night. For me, it demonstrated what I have learnt and applied in my life. I knew that I embodied the necessary strength and stillness to bring forth the safety and trust that those children needed at that moment, ensuring they could perform to their highest ability at that time. And I knew that I too, could trust the method being taught and allow the children to find their own way into themselves, to draw upon their own strength and confidence to fulfil their tasks.

This demonstrated to me, how I could bring forth the Gifts and Boons I had gained from my journey and bring them back into the Known World, in service to the community. I was doing so in a classroom of grade 5 students, and the benefits were palpable and profound.

Thank you to Nathalie Brewer for developing this wonderful transformational Yellow Lantern public speaking program for children.

Rewards, Boons and Gifts

Having survived the crises of the Journey it is vital that you bring your learnings back into the world. This is the application of the experience gained from your journey. It is essential that this experience is not just to benefit yourself, but is in service to the wider community, for the betterment of all. This is how the world is changed for the better.

The Rewards of your Journey may show up as a new perspective on life, a new appreciation and gratitude for yourself and your circumstances, or it may come in the form of new wealth, new relationships and new opportunities.

We have all heard many times the tales of those who have survived life-threatening illnesses or disasters, and afterwards say that that was the *best* thing that ever happened to them. This is because of the *depth* of their experience; it provided a catalyst to release old patterns and wounds, to open them to new awarenesses, and bring them a new sense of fulfilment and freedom. They now live in a whole new structure within themselves.

Rewards often come wrapped in humility. The only way to access some of your greatest gifts and your underlying character, is to endure and emerge from hardship. One of the challenges of this stage of your journey is finding ways to apply these new gifts. To do so, you may face challenges in the workplace, in social settings or relationships. You may need to step into a leadership role or adopt a new communication style, like listening more and telling less, or perhaps responding differently to situations of pressure and stress.

Temptations will also present themselves to challenge you to go back to old patterns and ways. For example, an old romantic relationship may return, or a job offer to go back for a lot more money, or someone from an old social group coming back into your life. These serendipitous situations show up so you can make decisions that show yourself and the universe that you are serious about who you truly are and who you have become. In these decisions, you are demonstrating your integrity, your values and your worth.

In my case, I had to learn how to apply new skills in my teaching career. Ten years into my career and the noise - the loud, loud cacophony of excited and chaotic classrooms of twenty-five ten-year-olds, created such pressure in my head and pain in my ears, that it would trigger a great angry reaction to get it to stop. My reaction would often scare the children into silence. At least for a minute or two.

Slowly, as I applied different techniques in the classroom and attended to my own healing, things in the classroom changed significantly. Many times, over the subsequent years, I have watched myself in a classroom with the same amount of chaos and noise and disruption, but I now experience the ability to navigate through it with a sense of calm and ease, even though it may still be painful in my ears. I don't get triggered into an angry tirade anymore.

Eventually, I bring a calm and settled state back into the classroom based on safety and enjoyment. It doesn't happen instantaneously, but it does happen, and the students know they are safe and accepted. And I feel the same way.

Rewards: The Gift of Sight

The Gift of Sight can show up by bringing you clarity. A clarity of vision of who you are and your life's purpose. You may then be able to create plans and inspire others who also share your vision or assist them in discovering their own vision and purpose. Ideas and projects associated with these visions may then emerge or be born from it. This could be as simple as finding methods of creative expression in music, art, dance, or writing, or perhaps creating business plans or innovative solutions to problems in your field of interest.

A gift of sight can also be about *seeing* other people's gifts and talents. It can mean nurturing or mentoring someone else's skills and abilities, or just letting them know you appreciate who they are and what they bring into the world. By *seeing* someone in this way, you act as a catalyst for bringing out their inherent genius.

Your sight could also expand into being able to *see* and be aware of different forms of energy and light. This means increased sensitivity and awareness to an expanded view of the universe and your world. Many people have increased psychic and spiritual abilities or sensitivities to nature after coming through their journey.

Others have new sensitivities to light and sound. Noises and music that previously seemed enjoyable, are now not. You may be more aware of the effects of different foods and behaviour patterns on your body. You may also be more aware of the different kinds of vibrations people emanate. Some people may radiate an energy of acceptance and confidence whilst others emit qualities of bitterness, blame and anger. This gift of sight may then lead you to decide where you would like to spend your time, money and energy, including relationships, places of work or recreation.

There is also the **Gift of *In-Sight***. *Insight* is a gift of finding heightened meaning and understanding about a thing or happening, which can lead to *seeing* underlying truths, as well as the inner character of people and relationships. In doing so, you access your well-spring of intuition, compassion and wisdom. This can be a very challenging gift, as others may not be ready to see, hear or know about these truths themselves.

By sharing your insights, you not only expand *your* awareness and clarity of thought, but you also create a pathway for others to do the same. Insight also provides greater awareness of your inner blockages and outer impediments to your growth and development. This means you can attend to your own healing with greater lucidity and efficacy, making your progress easier and more profound.

Rewards: The Gift of Balance

The Gift of Balance is a great reward to bring into your life, especially in this time of profound change and transformation. This means you bring awareness of your state of being in the moment. You are aware of your emotions, your thoughts, your body and your ability to communicate flexibly.

When you embody *balance,* you walk more easily between the different worlds in your life. You become a mediator between the worlds of spirit and nature, work and home, soulful purpose and ordinary obligations. Balance brings a stable influence and flexibility in your communication style, allowing others to move through their different states of emotion and thinking more easily, ensuring a level of harmony, even in times of discord.

People who have the gift of balance are alright with operating at a slower and steadier pace when necessary. They are not as excitable by circumstances, and their breath and their heartbeat are at a slower and deeper pace. This ensures they can both participate in and observe situations at the same time, often providing insightful and astute feedback.

Rewards: The Gift of Discernment

Discernment is a powerful gift. It brings forth an ability to *see* and then decide. It is both the sword and the heart of Christ Consciousness. A discerning person can *see* into motivations, issues and concerns with detached compassion and make decisions accordingly. It is the application of wisdom.

The Gift of Discernment means you can participate in highly charged emotional discussions, *and* still be present with good understanding and judgement. It means you remain aware of your own emotions and those around you, and can stay open with your thinking, your heart and your behaviour.

Remember, emotion leads thought and leads behaviour. But highly charged emotion shuts down and restricts someone's ability for rational thought and behaviour.

Someone with the Gift of Discernment brings sharp perception and nuanced judgements in making decisions from an open and detached point of view, rather than a closed one.

Rewards: The Gift of Inner Strength

Hidden power and talents are revealed through the gaining of inner trust. Qualities like resilience, asking for help, compassion, gratitude, setting boundaries and committing to inner truths, all emerge through your journey. These qualities are given added depth through the hardships you have endured through the abyss stage.

Your inner strength provides you with the capacity to accept your inner guidance and your intuition. Your inner strength can also be seen and trusted by others, who may then accept their inner guidance and intuition. This becomes quite apparent with someone who completes a cycle of healing.

Inner strength also allows for the **Gift of Not-Knowing**. Inner trust and inner strength allow a person to move through the stage of *not knowing*, of being uncertain about outcomes and unsure of how to resolve situations or circumstances. They allow themselves to relax and trust within this environment, even though it may be deeply uncomfortable. They know that sometimes situations just cannot be resolved, and the desired outcomes cannot be achieved at that time.

Sometimes, "I don't know", *is* the answer at that time. This can be very frustrating and painful to hear, especially in a relationship. This is especially so for women to hear a man express uncertainty or say they don't know how they feel or what to do. It is even more disconcerting when what you are wanting to hear, is reassurance and security. Yet not knowing, and saying you don't know, can be an act of great courage in the face of high expectation and pressure.

Rewards: The Gift of Maturity

The Gift of Maturity brings together all the other gifts within you. This is where you experience the intrinsic value of yourself and the way of the world. You can bring wisdom into your daily life. You can bring a grounded sense of strength and awareness into different situations because you have embodied the learnings from your journey. Using your insight, you can then discern what the appropriate action or judgement might be.

This is the embodiment of the wise Queen or King archetype. You are activating your sovereignty. You can, not only take responsibility for yourself, but also be aware of your responsibility in maintaining the health and good functioning of your wider 'realm', that is, your family, your workplace, and your community.

By creating this inward strength and ease, this inner-referencing, you provide the conditions for others to make their own decisions and live their own lives. This means you can allow others to make their own mistakes, as well as hold them accountable and responsible for those decisions and actions. A mature person, who stands in their sovereignty, is a powerful person who can listen, observe, provide counsel and take action where needed.

All these gifts come from your willingness, to not only go on your journey and discover your learnings and complete your soul contracts, but also to have the humility and awareness to bring them into the world, for the betterment of all. This is the culmination of the Hero's Journey.

The Gifts of the Mature Orphan Archetype

The final stages of your transformation are inherent within the Orphan archetype. This is where you confront your sense of abandonment, victimhood, anger, grief, and powerlessness, and emerge as an independent being of strong character and judgement.

This is where you bring your awareness and compassion into yourself, rather than looking 'out there' for your hope, purpose, love, affection, validation, and connection. You can now walk into the *golden shadow* or the mature aspect of the Orphan archetype. That is, those parts of yourself that you have not seen or valued that bring forth trust, gratitude, joy and appreciation, now come to the fore. This mature aspect has developed through you healing your core wounds, forgiving those who hurt you, and embracing community rather than shunning it.

The mature Orphan leads inevitably to you regaining sovereignty over yourself and your purpose. It leads to activating the Sovereign or King/Queen archetype within you.

What the Orphan confronts in you, is the ways in which you have abandoned yourself by directing your attention, intentions and energy, 'out there'. It calls forth your desire to withdraw from family, from intimacy in relationships, and the collegiate atmosphere of a workplace. It draws upon your sensitivities and neediness for the approval and judgement of others, bringing forth either resistance or compliance.

Orphans often look for a surrogate family. Because of their sense of abandonment, they look for comfort and affirmation outside of themselves. This is illustrated beautifully in the Pinocchio story, where Pinocchio finds his 'tribe' in the 'Lost Boys'.

The story shows how Orphans band together with like-minded, like-clothed people and call them 'my tribe'. This is where the Wounded Child within you, that hurt and wounded part, finds solace, connection and power amongst others who are similarly wounded.

The shadow side of the Orphan often displays itself in adolescent behaviours and attitudes. This is the shadow Rebel, exemplified in behaviours such as: rudeness, disrespect, bullying, argumentativeness, knowing 'everything', risk-taking, seeking hyper-stimulation or experiencing boredom to the point of being catatonic, and feeling injustice personally (*It's not fair!*). Adolescence though is an essential stage in the journey to adulthood.

But it is not only teenagers who express these behaviours, adults do the same thing, they just do it in more sophisticated and expensive ways. They are all simply different methods of avoidance. They become Wounded Child adults. As someone once said, 'Adults are just children, with better excuses.'

These are all aspects of the way of suffering on the path to freedom. This always ends at the door of humility. Humility is the place where you finally surrender and accept the love and gratitude that is your due and your right. You finally accept that your willpower and desire are not enough to change the world. It is only possible in your surrender, your openness, your vulnerability and finally your gratitude.

Your gratitude is that place where you are able to say, "Thank you", to yourself and the world for delivering you on your life-path. You can then finally breathe...and breathe easily without the restrictions of armour or defence. "Thank you", you whisper. "Thank you."

This is when your ego stops directing you and becomes your servant. Your ego is then serving your greater and higher Self in pursuing its grand life-purpose. This is the *golden shadow* of the Orphan. She/he is leading you to a greater appreciation of yourself, and a willingness to now enter into community with all of your gifts and share them in gratitude.

Trusting your Self

Trusting your Self is one of the highest and most courageous achievements you can accomplish in your life. It serves one of your main purposes in life: maturity.

It is truly not about how many Vipassanas you attend, whether you go on an ayahuasca journey, or how organic your diet is. It is about listening and attending to your Self. What is your Self telling you or asking of you at this time?

When you stop and listen, you demonstrate love and care to yourself. By doing so, you create space for acceptance and healing. It is this simple exercise that brings changes to your life. And when you change, when you heal and bring love to your Self, you change the world.

Sometimes the decisions you make as a result of your listening can lead you on pathways of pain, disruption and heartache. But this too is part of your journey. It may lead you to uncover the undigested trauma within your body and field. This is yours to transmute. It is then your willingness to attend to these energies - the Shadow and the Dark - *safely* (often with the assistance of experienced guides), that fulfils your Soul's mission and purpose. And in doing so, you fulfil your life's purpose.

The Gift of Patience

"Patience, patience, bloody patience", he thought loudly to himself. "The Gift of Patience is...more patience", he thought.

He drew a deep breath in, tightened his jaw, ground his teeth and sneered cynically. *"Yeah, yeah, yeah, I know, I've got to be more patient. 'It's a primary principle to live by', so they say. Patience, bloody patience."*

He loudly drew in his breath, sighed audibly, pursed his lips tightly and took a sip of his now stale-smelling, lukewarm cappuccino.

Another cynical sneer moved across his face just as a young mother and her child walked into the waiting room. The girl was whimpering and snivelling, all red eyes, red nose, snuffly and needy.

"Patience, yeah patience", he drew a deep breath in and sighed.

What A Miracle Looks Like - It's Very Ordinary

I met Dave many years ago. His young son Noah had a condition that meant he would have seizures, sometimes several a day, leaving him exhausted, in pain, and physically and mentally bruised.

One time, I saw Dave looking very agitated and angry. Noah had had a seizure that afternoon, and Dave was filled with anger from watching the aftermath of what the condition had done to his son. He was helpless. He could do nothing except watch and comfort his son afterwards. He was powerless, and so he raged.

"Who do you blame for this?", he was asked.

"Jesus Christ!", he answered through clenched teeth.

About three months later I saw Dave again, but this time he looked completely different.

"Ya know, I must be the luckiest man in the world," he said.

"Why is that?" I asked, rather perplexed as I remembered his state the last time I saw him.

"My son," he said. "I just spent a day with him, watching the birds at the wetlands".

He went on to explain how his son had looked up and pointed to one of the birds, saying, "Look at that Dad!"

The bird came into land on the lake, skidding to a stop, whilst another flapped and ran on top of the water to eventually take off. The boy was enraptured by these marvellous feats. A bird flying and landing, and another taking off and flying. Pretty ordinary stuff, Dave had seen it a thousand times or more.

Yet for Dave, it was like he was seeing the experience through his son's eyes, as if for the first time. He saw and experienced the wonder, the joy and the awe of something very ordinary: a bird taking off and landing.

Afterwards, even though nothing had changed about his son's condition or anything in his world at all, he became 'the luckiest man in the world!'

This, to me, is what a miracle looks like.

In the first instance, he intensely felt the pain, the suffering, and the unfairness of the world and what it was doing to his beautiful boy. And he was completely powerless and helpless, and so he raged.

He raged *out at* others. He raged against God and any power that had brought this suffering upon his son. And he despaired at his helplessness.

Then one day, with nothing changing 'out there', he experienced the wonderment of the world. *He* was changed. He was changed by his son helping him *see* what was right in front of him.

He changed his attitude and behaviour toward his wife too. His softening enabled her softening, which enabled them both to be more open and vulnerable about their own pain with each other. This enabled greater healing within her, and then between each other.

Most people want to change the world. They want to stop the suffering and unfairness in the world. They put **enormous** efforts into changing other people and things 'out there'. They rage and roar against the identified enemy (the coal industry, the chemical companies, the meat-eaters, the school system, the media, the Cabal, etc). And there is always, *always* another unfairness and injustice to fight. Their fights never end.

But it seems that the fight does end when you experience the transformation within yourself. This becomes the miracle that changes and heals the world. It's right in front of you. It's right within you, and it's very ordinary.

Unexpected Gifts

Oftentimes when you attend a workshop or a retreat, you receive unexpected gifts. There is someone there who says or does something, that quite unexpectedly, brings you an insight, an awareness, an opening, an opportunity, or a joy. It's most often not a material thing, but rather something that touches you or moves you into appreciation. This happened to me in 2019 when I attended a meditation retreat at Mt Mellum in the Sunshine Coast hinterland (extraordinary location and venue - a gift in itself), where I received at least five gifts from different people.

During my morning preparations, I received an unexpected cryptic message from a dear friend. Her message was a portent of future ventures and success, and encouragement to continue trusting myself and follow my path. It was an unexpected gift and pathway to appreciation, and I smiled with an expectation of what was to come.

When I arrived, I chose my spot to sit, and after a little while started a conversation with the bloke next to me. In answering the question, "What attracted you to this retreat?", he responded with profound themes of a life-path similar to mine. He had worked in teaching and assisted people in life transition. He had also been a priest. There was an immediate resonance for me. "Ha!", I said to myself, "My second gift". *I am not alone. I am not the only one.* "Mmmm... thank you", I said to myself.

At the break, I turned to the woman on the other side of me. Her name was unusual, mysterious and quite beautiful. It was a name I knew I had heard before as a character in a book I had recently read. I asked her what her name meant, and she said, "Mediator". And inwardly, I again took a deep breath in. That's an important archetype for me. You see, only about three weeks ago I drew some archetype cards and drew... the Mediator.

The Mediator archetype has a deep and rich resonance, as it not only describes qualities of someone who is able to listen and respect the different perspectives of others, but someone who can also move between worlds and feel comfortable in each region. It also speaks of the alchemical notion of 'As Above, So Below', as well as the Greek God Hermes, and the Crow as a spirit animal. Mmmm... another gift. "Thank you", I said again.

During the break, all participants were chatting with each other. I spoke with a lovely woman who lived in Maleny, a town fifteen minutes away. Again, I took a deep breath in; I had been drawn to Maleny for the past four years or so, as a place I would love to live. But not only that, she was a friend of the friend who sent me the message that morning! Ha! That was funny! A lovely synchronicity. And yes, you guessed it, another gift.

After the break, we continued with the meditations, all of which were rich and wonderful. Finally, the retreat ended, and we went on our way back home.

On the way home, I stopped at a roadside veggie shop, wanting to get some fruit for dinner. There was fresh local produce for sale: lychees, pawpaw, cantaloupe, and cherry tomatoes. A wonderful cornucopia of local foods.

I was waiting at the checkout behind a young hippy couple who had purchased a potpourri of produce. Quite unexpectedly a local woman asked them if they would like to try some *'miracle fruit'*. "It's a miracle for yer taste buds", she said. She gave them two red seeds from a plant which grows in her yard. She gave them strict instructions about what to do, "Swish it around yer mouth and around yer tongue. But don't swallow the pips!", she said.

The veggie shop owner, who had obviously seen this play out several times before, bemusedly cut up a lime for them to eat.

"Eat the lime", she said, "Don't just swallow the juice. Eat it. What should be sour will be sweet. That's the miracle."

Well, the next fifteen minutes or so was this couple going through an ecstatic awareness of their senses as the shop owner gave them some pineapple, an apple, an orange, and finally a passionfruit to eat and experience this new sensation.

"Ohhhh ... wow! Ohhhh... amazing... the lime is so sweet! It's incredible."

The local woman then asked me if I would like to try them. Of course, I said, "Yes". I too experienced a reorientation of my taste sensations, experiencing common fruits as if for the first time. Wow, what a gift!

During this time, the young man and I started chatting. He and his partner had just come from a yoga retreat up the road a bit. I spoke to him of the gifts I had received at my retreat, and he especially picked up on the Mediator archetype and the god Hermes. He pulled up his shirt and pointed to an enormous tattoo of a caduceus on his back, the symbol of Hermes. By the way, tattoos are big up there, and big tattoos are really *big* up there!

A *caduceus* is the traditional symbol of the Staff of Hermes, featuring two snakes winding around a winged staff. The column of the staff represents stability, the snakes entwined around it represent the harmony of different energies, as well as renewal and intelligence. The wings represent the ability to move to different positions, as well as being able to fly into the spirit world and be grounded by the staff at the same time. This had great significance for me. A symbol for the qualities I will embody as the Mediator. Another brilliant gift in conversation and connection. "Thank you", I said again, "Thank you".

And so, it was a day of gifts. Gifts were given and received, and all moving me to a place of appreciation and gratitude. Thank you to all.

What is Sacred?

What is sacred? What is a sacred place? How do you know that's what it is?

You know it because of the stillness. Because of the certainty that is inherent within it. You know it because it aligns with the certainty and the stillness that is inherent within *you*.

It is the stillness that brings power and attraction. It is not in wanting and demanding, planning and believing. The stillness enables the connection between the earth and your spirit. It connects the depth of your soul, that earthy, grounded base of strength within you, to the boundless expanse of the world of spirit.

You are the conduit of the sacred. You bring the sacred to life and emanate it in your being and bring it into the world. You become the divine walking here on earth, wherever you are, whoever you are with. You are the sacred element in this life, and you emanate that in your life, now.

Connecting to the Greater Source

Connecting to the greater source of all things has been with humans for eons.

Cultures from all across the world have told stories, created art, sculptures and painted images of their connection to this force for thousands of years.

They depicted their connection with nature, with natural forces, with the cycles of the earth, and with the stars and heavenly beings. And this was a natural and normal part of their lives. This connection was present in all aspects of their lives.

So too now, with this enforced quiet because of the coronavirus lockdown, has allowed many people to move back into connection.

For some, this disruption has caused intense stress and grief. Their minds and emotions have become so overwhelmed they must create stories around these feelings to enable their expression. Hence, people create conspiracies to bring a sense of certainty and control over their world.

STAGE 6: THE ROAD BACK - REWARDS AND GIFTS

And people love stories. And people love scary stories. The scarier the better.

And people think too much. And they believe their thoughts. This adds to the anxiety and fear. And some people find this state of distress, comforting, because it brings certainty and a sense of control.

But this too shall pass.

There is a much bigger movement going on creating connections, at high levels of vibration, amongst a vast group of humanity across the world.

They are not an elite group. They are ordinary people who can embody this connection to nature and the heavens in their ordinary lives. They might work on your car, make you a coffee, clean your house, have a healing business, drive a bus, grow your food or teach your kids. Just ordinary stuff.

And they are connected. And they have done the work.

So, finding the way of connection to this greater force during this time is an act of meditation. You are the mediating link between heaven and earth, between the mystery and material reality.

Intuition is the feedback you receive from it.

Acting upon that intuition embodies the grace of the universe in this moment right now. And it is done in very ordinary ways.

And it is enacted through ordinary heroes who bring this connection into the world right now. Thank you.

Questions and Exercises:

1. Give some thought as to when, where and how you experienced 'The Return' and 'The Road Back' in your life.
   - Name two occasions when you know you experienced a Return.
   - What were the gifts and the pressures the Return brought to you?
   - What 'triggered' the Road Back?
   - What archetypes did the Road Back bring up for you? Eg: the Hero, the Saboteur, the Healer, the Magical Child, the Prostitute, the Rescuer, the Teacher, the Warrior etc?
2. Looking back, what three things do you think you were supposed to learn from the Return?
3. How did you respond to the various trials and challenges you were presented during your Road Back? Name two that you know you responded well to, and two that you know you didn't respond well.
4. What pressures were upon you to make decisions during your Road Back?
   - How did you make your decisions?
   - Did you respond with grandiosity or with humility and clarity?
5. Name at least three Gifts and Rewards you have gained through your journey?
6. Name three things from this part of the book that moved you or struck you as important.
7. Creative expression - drawing: Take some time to find a quiet space. Breathe deeply and relax your body. Feel the breath go all the way through your body, and clear your mind. With paper, coloured pencils or crayons in front of you, ask yourself clearly, "Show me what is important for me to know from this part of the book."

   Then, with your non-dominant hand, choose a pencil or crayon, and start drawing. It doesn't matter what it looks like, just create. Change hands when your body tells you. Repeat.

Stage 7: Reintegration

Having been through great ordeals of loss, illness and devastation, the Hero (You) has arisen into new strength, capability, and awareness. You have reconciled with the forces within and those outside of you, both your light and your shadow sides. And you have found the way to walk between these worlds.

And of course, the challenges do not cease. Before returning to the Known World, there may be unforeseen ordeals you encounter. This final threshold provides one last test or temptation to solidify your growth. In this final stage, You (the Hero) can become master of both worlds, with the freedom to live and grow, and to influence your community broadly.

Returning with your gifts and talents, you experience life differently. You are no longer a naive child or rebellious adolescent seeking excitement or adventure. You are now comfortable with yourself, having evolved through your challenges to become an expanded being, capable of handling new responsibilities and challenges.

That Moment of In-Between

After your great ordeals and challenges, there is a time of in-between. It is the time after the Destroyer has rampaged through your life, clearing and purging and eliminating all that is not aligned with your new divine Self.

You may have got rid of friends from Facebook, eliminated clothes from your wardrobe, left a job, gone through a cleansing dietary regime or gone through the immensity of the Abyss and Rebirth process. It is all about getting rid of that which is not aligned with your new emerging Self.

Just as the Destroyer has literally rampaged through the Australian landscape in 2019 and 2020, destroying untold millions of hectares and life-forms, out of the ashes, comes new life. It cannot be helped. It is a natural movement and awakening from the earth, up into the world. It is a Return into life and into the world.

And just like the rampant rains that spread their life-giving riches onto the landscape in the aftermath of the fires, so too do we allow for our feelings to come forth and cleanse us. Grief naturally emerges as we let go of the old.

After the fires, there was a wide experience of grief within the Australian community, for the massive loss in the landscape and within ourselves. You must allow for uncertainty in the wake of such destruction: what comes next? Who will I be in this new land?

Trust. Trusting your Self. Trusting your intuitive guidance. Trust that when the Call comes, you will know what to do, and how to act. You will know. You just will.

The Call may not match the images from your Vision Boards, or your Dream list, or your manifestation and co-creation list. It will just feel right, and you will know. You will just know.

So, follow your guidance and discern the difference between the call of your desires and wants (normally feelings of fear, scarcity and desire), and that of your Intuition.

The way of your intuition is stillness, and a quiet certainty. It is not a 'high-five' moment, it is just *knowing*.

So, listen. Attend. You will Know. Trust. Accept and allow. Everything is alright.

Obstacles Are Part of The Journey

Sometimes obstacles are just part of your journey in life. It doesn't mean you have done anything 'wrong'. All the great sages and prophets, like Yeshua (Jesus), Gautama Buddha and Mahatma Gandhi, all experienced hardship and heartache.

To take a more noble view of life, what if the 'obstacles' were a sign that you are actually 'on purpose' in your life? And by enduring them and surviving, you are helping transmute those forces for all? Obstacles can then be a sign of the divine living *in* the world; not of its absence.

The way of love and life is often to creatively destroy old ways and patterns of thinking, perceiving and being. This is one of the hardest stages of growth to go through.

But the way of nature is to create new life out of the remnants of the old. Even in toxic environments, nature creates new forms and ways of life.

As humans, our essence of life is to endure and create. We can move through times of desolation, of complete and utter loss and emptying, and, after a period of recuperation, in which it appears that 'nothing' is happening, new growth, new awareness and a new being emerges.

This is the importance of the times we live in now. The revolution doesn't occur 'out there', but within. It is a revolution that allows the old armour of your thinking, plans, demands and defences, your old structure, to be released and let go. You don't need all that energy tied up in all that stuff anymore. It is truly the time to step into your vulnerability and allow the power of love and nature to fill the void created.

Surviving Through a Crisis

Yeah, I was there. I was there during the great toilet paper crisis in Australia of March 2020. Yeah, I survived. I got through.

We had to resort to some pretty ingenious ways to clean our bums... but we got through.

At first, we used hand-towels, but there was potential to clog up the pipes. Then we resorted to newspapers and old notebooks... but same problem.

STAGE 7: REINTEGRATION

Artist: Alden Maben

We needed a radical solution. We didn't have enough tissue paper, so that wasn't a viable option, and my flatmate had just had a big bowl of chicken curry... so we needed a solution and fast.

The hippy next door suggested hemp. "Hemp", he said, "Good for the environment and soft on yer bum cheeks too. And if you eat some of it before you go, it will cure yer cancer, heal yer skin problems, and make yer feel good all at the same time."

I told him he was dreamin'. I thought he'd been smokin' something.

And Hodgey across the road had the idea of using grass. Didn't turn out well. He got big red rashes on his bum, and dogs started followin' him round.

One good thing though, the local nurse had to come round and put special ointment on his bum and in his crack. They're married now. That saying's true that love comes out of pain.

And then my flatmate hit it... water. Use water to clean yer bum. Radical man, radical.

So, no more paper waste being flushed down our dunny! We went old school... we used our hands and water!

And yes, we survived... no-one shakes my hand anymore... but hey, I'm right with social distancing protocols, and sometimes yer gotta make sacrifices in a crisis.

No toilet paper, use water instead; clean bum, clean environment, clean mind. Everybody wins.

"I cannot deny, there is a great road in this life" - Shimamura Kojin (author of Jiro Monogatari - The Story of Jiro)

These were Kojin's final words and were written down for me by his son (then in his early seventies), to be presented to the Principal of the school I was working at in northern Japan.

'Jiro Monogatari' (The Story of Jiro) is one of **the** most famous books in Japan. I had been given a great honour in receiving these words, and I appreciate them and their meaning more so now, as I begin the beginning of a new stage of my life.

We all have a 'great road' to follow in this life, it's just that mostly we don't know what it is, until we get to the end of a stage. Then we can look back and see how all that stuff we went through actually served a purpose.

This is why I love the Hero's Journey so much. It allows for times of success and failure, of hardship, heartache, and turmoil and eventually for the transcendence of these circumstances, into a new journey. A journey in which the maturity and insight gained from the past can be utilised in service for the benefit of all.

I have witnessed many people go through times of great struggle as they quite desperately try to hold onto the certainties of their past successes and identities. Their ego, which has kept them safe and successful through past times, doesn't want them to let go of these successful formulas. It may then show up in *shadow* form because it wants so desperately to create the world the way *it* wants it to be, not the way that it actually is.

So, what happens when your 'great road' takes an unexpected turn away from the familiar road, onto a decidedly 'chaotic' and uncertain path?

This path is often described as the 'road into darkness', and it is essential in your spiritual and temporal progression and maturity. It is a road which leads to the stripping away of all that you once knew and held dear, of all your identities and certainties, and leaves you in a hellish realm with only your fears, desperations and despairs to keep you company.

This is the breakdown of the old. It must happen so that a new, more complex structure of both higher and greater depth, can be created.

The 'Great Road' leads you in, and then leads you out. Even if you make decisions based on fear or desire for the old, the Great Road will lead you out.

It shows you that your decisions don't determine your outcomes, as that has already been decided. Rather it shows you that your decisions determine the level of comfort you experience on your journey.

This is where you can choose to partner the Fool or the Trickster archetypes, who are familiar and comfortable with disruption, chaos and disorder.

The Trickster knows that disruption is part of the journey and enjoys creating it and revelling in it. The Fool can hear and see the wisdom in this process, and can find a way to laugh, without bypassing, ensuring the integration of the experience into your body and being.

Both the Trickster and the Fool allow for the humbling of the Warrior, the Hero, and the Victim. This is essential. The shadow side - the arrogance, disconnection, righteousness and neediness - is confronted and humbled. This is what grounding looks like.

As the Road leads you out, you are often presented with a temptation, attempting to take you back into the old. This is often a relationship, a job, or some other circumstance which immediately challenges your decision to change and move on. Some may experience this as an Icarus moment. That is, an experience that takes you too high too soon, that inevitably, leads to your downfall, your coming 'down-to-earth', with a painful crash.

In order to leave the hellish realm, a very alluring temptation comes along which says you can get out of your circumstances easily, just by doing these easy things You may experience some immediate success and feel elated, relieved or even ecstatic. But soon, you fly too high, move too far away from *your road*, and then you must experience a crashing-back-to-earth moment: the Fall. Some may go back into old responses for a short time. But the Road will only lead you back to the place of humbling again.

This is where you must put your new learnings and wisdom into action, and this will begin from the ground up. This is where seeds are sown for the harvest that will take place sometime further along the road.

This ending of endings is very challenging to those who already 'know' their purpose and are certain of their path. They are the ones who must give up the most and surrender to the way of their Great Road. But this of course, begins the beginning of the beginning; the time of hope, vision, and new purpose.

I too now know, that "I cannot deny, there is a great road in this life". Thank you, Shimura-san, for helping me with such a great lesson.

The Profound Purpose of a Beautiful Boy - The Dark Crystal

In the early morning of October 29, I received a call from my brother saying that his son, his beautiful 16-year boy, had died.

After the initial shock of the news and the sadness, I began to feel and reflect upon my nephew's life.

The Dark Crystal was Sean's favourite movie when he was a kid. I used to baby-sit him and my niece a lot when they were little. It was always a funny and enjoyable task. We used to play hide-and-seek, wrestle, and then sit down on the couch and watch a movie. Sean would always choose The Dark Crystal. He used to sit close to me with my arm around him as we watched. I think I must have seen it at least five or six times with him, but he probably watched it another forty or fifty more.

It is a profound tale of Jen, an orphan 'Gelfling', whose task it is to go on a quest to find the missing shard of a great crystal. He then must journey under the mountain-home of the dark forces, the Skeksis, and re-join the shard with the great Crystal, to bring balance back into the universe.

Jen encounters many trials and challenges along the way, which brings up his fears and insecurities. He must learn how to trust and work with others and accept their help when offered, to achieve the greater goal of restoring the great Crystal, and thereby, healing the world.

This, of course, was Sean's story too. He held a beautiful divine light around him until he was about eighteen months old. This was his core; his Great Crystal. But he had to go on a quest to find the missing shards brought on by his woundedness, and then reintegrate them within himself.

As he engaged with his missing pieces, he encountered dark forces that exaggerated his sense of woundedness, hurt and insecurities. He would lash out in blameful outbursts at the supportive forces around him, or bully those less powerful than him.

But his underlying confidence, sensitivity and creativity would often shine through as he often engaged with vulnerable others, the young and the disabled, in very caring and protective ways.

He was also very creatively destructive as he found ways to entertain himself. He would lie face down on his skateboard, paddle around like this for a while, dragging his feet behind him using his brand new sneakers as brakes. Doh!

He was also a very good-natured cheeky boy. He belonged to a farty family. They farted a lot and enjoyed farting on other people. When he was little and I was babysitting, he would sometimes jump onto my lap, do a fart, and then jump off and run-away giggling saying, "I just farted on you."

But Sean had a profound purpose to fulfil, much like that of Jen in the Dark Crystal. His job was to find ways to reconcile these dark and light forces within him. His task was to find the path to healing within, by reintegrating his missing shards (his woundedness and abandonment), by venturing under the dark mountain, and thereby restoring himself into wholeness and fulfilment.

He certainly had that capability. I can see him as 'That' guy who had been on the journey through the dark lands (anger, addiction, blame and insecurity), to emerge as a confident force of creativity, healing and balance, to guide other young men through their journey. I could see him working with rites of passage groups as one of their leaders.

He would be *that* guy, like in that most famous scene from Good Will Hunting, who knows, "It's not your fault." He would be the one who could hold other young men as they go through their journey through the dark lands and experience the upwelling of shame and guilt, as they acknowledge and then clear their untrue belief systems and structures.

But he was just a kid. He was only sixteen.

Interestingly, numerologically, Sean was a 12/3. The 1 being Creativity and Confidence. The 2, being Balance and Co-operation, that is, reconciling the forces within, to work with others to bring balance, harmony and restoration. And 3, his primary life force, being Expression and Sensitivity. Being able to feel his sensitivity, his creativity, and his desire for balance, and express it confidently, in co-operation with others, in the world.

But he was just a kid. All these big things swirling within him brought confusion and inner and outer conflict. Who to trust? What to do? How can he accept help?

And as much as he was a silly, angry, immature, destructive goof-ball, he was also a beautiful boy. A beautiful boy, with a profound purpose to live out.

May you be blessed, Sean. I know you are alright. I know you are with your spirit guides now, and you are laughing and smiling about what you have achieved here.

The Dark Crystal is a great movie and a wonderful reminder about how an ordinary person can have a profound mission in this life. Thank you, Sean. You are always loved.

'Negative' Feelings Aren't Always 'Bad'

What the 'positive development' and spiritual growth movements have done is to define what is 'positive' as 'good' and 'right', and what is 'negative' as 'wrong' and 'bad'.

What this has come to mean is that what is comfortable and timely, is seen as positive and good, and what is uncomfortable and inconvenient is negative or wrong. But it is not true.

The proliferation of 'Law of Attraction' and 'Twin Flame' articles, books and courses speak to the desire within many people to never experience hardship, discomfort, pain, or inconvenience. That is, a desire to never experience suffering. Yet suffering is an inherent part of our lives as human beings.

Having worked as a primary school teacher for many years, I would see daily, children reacting passionately to the unfairness they saw or experienced. They reacted loudly when someone didn't want to play with them, or they thought someone said nasty things about them. They reacted when they fell over, didn't do as well as they wanted to, or they couldn't have what they wanted when they wanted it. (Hmmm... *they couldn't have what they wanted, when they wanted it*.) They experienced suffering. And they didn't like it, and they didn't know how to deal with it.

Well, "adults are just children with better excuses", as the saying goes. Little did these children know, they were experiencing the gradual developmental process of maturity. That is, the inevitable realisation that the world is not perfect, that life is unfair, and the idealism of innocence must be lost for wisdom and maturity to arise. This is hard to come to terms with, even for adults.

I experienced depression, ill health and powerlessness for many years. I experienced many, many years of failure and experienced the consequences of my repressed shadow feelings and tendencies. When I learnt of the personal development movement's ideas that by setting goals and implementing plans, I could change my circumstances, I actively embraced and adopted their methods.

I actively used 'positivity', vision boards, goal setting and affirmations. I joined mastermind groups and hung out with people whom I wanted to be like. I did *all* the things I was supposed to do to change my circumstances and achieve 'success'. But it didn't happen. They didn't work. None of those 'positive' Law of Attraction methods worked for me.

At times, they seemed to make my depression and circumstances worse, because they asked me to deny the reality of what I was actually feeling and experiencing right now, which was disappointment, heartache and loss. But despite all my efforts, I was still experiencing my life's purpose, even though I wasn't getting what I wanted.

Now, so many years later, I see that time as a process and journey into Initiation and healing, and finally transmutation and fulfilment. I was able to see my journey as not one of failure, but one of trust and faith in myself, even when I made decisions that seemed wrong and painful at the time. I now deeply value my capacity for perseverance, persistence, and self-referencing through very difficult circumstances.

I found a way to engage with the hardship and my feelings, and I was able to acknowledge and integrate my Shadow self: my fear, anger, guilt and shame. It allowed me to move more fully into the expression of my true self more often. The 'negative' circumstances I experienced in my life, became a pathway to wholeness and healing.

Now I give thanks for that time as it showed me my underlying character and values. I now appreciate myself, my journey, and my life, even though I tried so very hard for it to be otherwise.

Just by Surviving, You Fulfil Your Purpose

Sometimes it's not about achieving your dreams, it's just simply about surviving; coming through a hard journey. Just doing this *is* achieving your soul's purpose.

So, what if your soul's purpose is to heal inter-generational issues? Your life then could be about absorbing dark and foul energies from generations past. And in your survival, you transmute them into higher-level vibrations of light. This is the true meaning of alchemy: following a process that transforms lower and heavy energies into gold. It's not pleasant, it's not sexy, but it is truly noble and heroic.

STAGE 7: REINTEGRATION

For many sensitive people, experiencing the harshness of the world, with all its conflict and injustice, is an extremely painful experience. These realities can take a huge toll on someone's mental, emotional and psychic well-being.

It takes its toll because your job in this lifetime is not about stopping or changing the world through your intellect, your will-power or your understanding, but through your feeling and surviving. Surviving your journey through feeling completes your soul contracts. By not suppressing or repressing your feelings, you allow yourself to feel and experience all that you need to. This is deep work, and truly courageous.

It is through this mechanism that you become the alchemist's vessel. That is, you endure the heat, the darkness, the pressure, the isolation, the separation and the destruction of old structures and known forms, to emerge finally, having been cleared of all previous vibrations, distilled to your essence, as a new form and being. You arise anew. This is transmutation. This is your power, your torment, and your freedom.

There are many distractions and temptations along this path. The many conspiracies that are now touted as truth are an example of this. They take your energy and attention away from within yourself and your areas of influence, into areas where you have no power at all. They get you focussed entirely 'out there' at 'them'. They are distractions from your primary soul work; that of feeling and taking responsibility for what is in your field.

But you do have power. You have power to influence and transform what is in your energy field. You have the power to acknowledge it, feel it, communicate with it, and transmute it. This *is* your power manifest in your being, here and now.

You also have the power to decide what you do now. Where do you put your attention and your energy? Into distractions, or do you attend to what is within you? And now that you have emerged, what is calling your attention now?

Just living your life, is fulfilling your purpose. By attending to your soul contracts and completing them, as painful as that can be, you are fulfilling your purpose. By listening to your inner voice, your intuition, referencing yourself and learning how to love yourself, you are fulfilling a profound life purpose.

Career and business, money and relationships, are all a normal part of your life, but they are not your purpose. Your purpose is about fulfilling your soul contracts, and then bringing your gifts and talents and wisdom into your life. This can be through a business, a career, and relationships. But it is by applying these gifts and your wisdom, that you embody and demonstrate your purpose.

The mature embodiment of your essence and its application in your life is some of the hardest, most ordinary, and most profound things you can do in your life. This is the way of the Courageous Vulnerable, and it is an heroic journey to live it out.

Relationships and Purpose

For me, it seems that my life is not about being in a romantic partnership. This circumstance has made me feel at times like I am either doing something wrong, or there is something wrong with me. I realise now that I am alright, and this is just the way my life has been during this period.

What makes life more painful is when you compare yourself to others and what they have, rather than valuing and living your own life.

For most of my life, it has been about living alone, with not much money or any form of success in career or relationship. Now, however, I know and value the journey I have been on, and know that all of what I have experienced, is fulfilling my life's purpose.

I don't know your circumstances, or what is right for you, but I do know that your life's purpose is often far greater, and far more ordinary than what you want, or believe it should be.

Attracting Recurring Patterns

Those times when I was seeking a relationship though, I found that I was attracting a *lot* of wounded women. I understand what this cycle was about now, and don't need to repeat that sort of drama anymore.

I now understand that I was playing out, quite unconsciously, my desire to fulfil my role as a Rescuer or Healer or wanting validation for my own Woundedness. So, I was presented, often very loudly, with a beautiful

"You go through challenges in your marriage and there's a reward at the end of it. There's this incredible reward, that you love each other more. You learn something. You let go of something. Those hard edges get softened. You are that block of stone, and life shapes you and takes away those hard edges."

**Olivia Harrison, in relationship
with George Harrison for 30 years.**

Victim, right in front of me. I then had the opportunity to try to 'heal' her or rescue her from her circumstances.

I have also tried being the Servant to women who embody a Shadow Princess archetype and have realised that that doesn't work either. The Shadow Princess is the immature version of the Queen. They feel very entitled, are self-centred and demanding. Nothing, absolutely nothing I did was ever good enough or appreciated. In fact, after I had done all that she had asked or demanded of me, she was even more pissed-off because now she had nothing to complain about!

Eventually, I learnt that I couldn't make someone else change or heal them or make them happy, whether with service, kindness, logic or love. That was their job.

I realised I couldn't make someone change with demands or emotional pleas either; they change in their own time, and in their own way. And that's the hard part. It takes patience and acceptance to be in a relationship.

I also realised that I couldn't make someone see me, appreciate me or understand me. That's my job. My job is to go on my journey to gain all these gifts and say the words of appreciation and love that only I can say to myself. "I see you. I appreciate you, and I love you."

This stage showed me how the desire to be seen and heard by someone else, to be valued and appreciated, to be held and comforted, and to be loved, fills a primal need within us. It is a universal desire. It is especially difficult as a sensitive, empathic person, as you don't like witnessing others going through difficult and painful journeys. You want others to be healed and strong, as this then releases the tension you feel within yourself.

But your journey to self-love is a universal one. It is a profound transformation, and no-one else can do it for you. It is your own Hero's Journey into the courageousness of your vulnerability.

Your Thoughts Don't Create Your Life

Your thoughts do not create your life. Your thoughts help you understand your life... eventually. And your feelings show you how you are responding to your life.

STAGE 7: REINTEGRATION

All people go through difficult and uncomfortable times sometime in their life. This is normal. This *is* your life's journey. It is a journey into maturing. It is a journey to fulfil soul contracts that were made before you were born. This is a profound and purposeful life.

Your maturing means you can experience your life, endure hardships and turmoil, and emerge with wisdom and meaning, rather than cynicism and bitterness. You will feel fulfilled and content from your journey because you have engaged with it fully in your life.

There is much more to life and its creation than just your thoughts, despite what some spiritual texts, self-development and positive-thinking proponents may suggest. There is a mystery going on, far more profound and complex than what you think, know, or understand at the time.

Nature is not personal. The storm that wreaks havoc through a community doesn't pick out the mean people or the ones with 'negative' thoughts to only destroy their properties. It follows its own path, influenced by bigger forces than we can see from our human perspective. It is not personal.

It is true that you are an energy being, and you live both in a quantum world of swirling paradoxical forces and energies, and at the level of dense matter, at the same time.

Thoughts are energy and so they do interact within the quantum field, yes, that is true. But then, so do your feelings, the archetypes you embody, and the different layers within your energetic field. And most importantly, so does your soul.

Your soul wants you to fulfil your soul contracts. This has a profound effect upon the quantum field, to bring the people and circumstances you need to fulfil and complete the contracts you agreed to before you were born.

Your conscious awareness is only a very small part of your field. Therefore, much of what happens to you on your Journey, is due to unconscious patterns unfolding, clearing and resolving. This is why, the circumstances that come to you in your life, mostly, have nothing to do with your conscious thought. You cannot be aware of it because you are unconscious of it. As Carl Jung, the famous psychologist said, "The unconscious is really unconscious."

It seems to me then, that these other factors have far more influence over your circumstances than merely your thoughts. Even Wayne Dyer, the well-known author and spiritual teacher, had problems and issues that he found difficult to deal with. And even Anthony Robbins, the famous self-help author, doesn't always get his goals.

So rather than trying to control your life through your thoughts (which is really hard), it is easier to allow your life to unfold, and follow your intuition and inner guidance to achieve your life's greater goals and purpose.

This will lead to a life in alignment with your soul's purpose. And that is simply, a courageous path to follow.

A Bigger Movement at Play

I have noticed a big movement at play around the world over the last decade or so. The Destroyer is at work creating space for new awareness to come into the consciousness of humanity. But as old paradigms and states of awareness break down, it is accompanied by an eruption of energy and emotion as a response to, or a reaction against this new structure.

It is easy to see an underlying anger, righteousness and blame being expressed across communities around the world. There are protests about the environment, women's rights, democracy being subverted, refugees and great humanitarian crises caused by wars and drugs.

No more so than within the spiritual and activist communities. Many have moved into the Conspiracy Community declaring their awareness of all the terrible earth-destroying plots and schemes being implemented by 'the Cabal' and other nefarious groups and individuals. This is a demonstration of how people's attention and energy can be manipulated, hijacked and distracted. These conspiracies get people focussed 'out there' away from your internal sources of power and reference. This is what a Temptation looks like on the Hero's Journey.

Its purpose is to distract you and take you away from your higher purpose of discovering your gifts and applying them in the world.

Yet there is a bigger movement at play. These eruptions of emotion and ego must come out, they must be felt and expressed. It would be best of course, if this were done safely, within healing ceremonies or rituals, where a sacred vessel could be created to hold and then transmute these energies. But this is not happening. It is being expressed loudly as people gravitate into polarised, tribal groups.

So, having done your work and gained your gifts and wisdom, how do you respond?

Having done your work and integrated your learnings and new energies, you are far more capable and competent in enduring, and transmuting these blasts from others. You have the capacity now to witness these emotional expressions without them touching you so personally. Many people around the world have grown and matured powerfully during this time of transition, enabling them to be the catalysts and vessels for transformation and healing.

We are in a final stage of change and growth, an 'end-of-days' so to speak, and these eruptions are manifestations of that. This is what ascension looks like. It is not about leaving the planet, but rather, bringing a higher vibration into the earth plane, and then integrating and embodying it. This is what it means to 'bring heaven to earth'.

May all those who are close to these vast emotional outbursts be blessed and stay safe as you go through your journey. Know that you are not the cause of these expressions. But rather, the means by which these lower level and denser energies are transformed and transmuted. You are the Alchemist. A great gift to the world. Thank you.

Crossing the Threshold, Again

> *"Before enlightenment, chop wood and carry water.*
> *After enlightenment, chop wood and carry water."*
>
> **Zen Buddhist saying.**

Whatever you achieve in your life, it is important to carry on doing the basics that ensure health and well-being. Politeness, self-care, empathy, appreciation and gratitude are all basic elements that ensure you are embodying 'enlightenment', and therefore bringing more of the divine into your life and into the world.

Enlightenment also means that doing your ordinary tasks in life (*chopping wood and carrying water*), are not done from a sense of obligation, superiority or martyrdom. These ordinary tasks, like taking the kids to school, doing the dishes, words of appreciation to your partner or lover, or paying the bills are all part of your normal earthly life. These simple tasks can also be infused with enlightened good intention, love and care, if you pay attention and allow it.

This is a process of listening and attending to your inner calling and your intuition. It is attending to the needs of your Soul. Your soul is not just calling you from within yourself, but also calling to you from within the earth. It is calling you to ground, align and integrate your energy and awareness. This is bringing 'heaven to earth', by bringing your gifts and wisdom into your ordinary life.

Although many people believe that enlightenment is the endpoint and achievement of their spiritual quest and seeking, it is just the movement into another state of awareness. Once achieved, its purpose is not to stay in that revered heavenly state amongst the Masters, but to embody this fully, and bring it into your daily life. Bring it into the community. This is the culmination of the Hero's Journey, and it is how you change the world, by embracing the nobility of the ordinary.

Enlightenment is about bringing yourself fully into the world and attending to what presents itself in your daily life. It is as easy and as difficult as that.

Emptying the Old and Integrating the New

It seems that there are a *lot* of people going through similar states of change and upheaval right now. Relationships, jobs, and where people live are all changing. People are emptying, moving on and allowing something new to come in.

There is a collective restructuring of our fields going on. There is an emptying of the old, an infusion and integration of the new, so this new structure can be applied in the world.

Be the Grounded Vessel

Be the grounded vessel.
The anchoring point.
The one who provides security and surety for others.
The stable one.

Be the knowing that comes from wholeness:
The beingness that radiates
Health,
Safety,
Wisdom.
Be the Healer and the Carer.
The one who nurtures and grows.
The one who provides sustenance,
And the richness of protection.
The one who transforms.
The catalyst.
Be the grounded vessel.
The one who loves,
All ways.

When you know you are coming to the end of a cycle, it is very useful to look back with appreciation for where you have been. Even the hardest and darkest of times can bring great rewards and learnings if you allow it.

We seem to have nearly completed our journeys of healing and transmutation of those old, dark and unhealthy energies. These old soul contracts are now complete. We are now moving into a new relationship with the world and ourselves, based on a new realisation of our inherent divine selves.

The movement from one dimension of being to the next, means we leave behind *all* that we believed that was once so important from that previous dimension.

Many people are leaving the old, with no new plan to go into. There is no new guaranteed job or house or relationship to go to. And although the uncertainty of their experience is acknowledged and felt keenly, they feel good. It is not the old feeling of desperation, crying out, or lashing out in fear and victimhood that is arising. There is a new calmness, a resilient strength of walking into the unknown, and knowing that, "I'm alright."

This is what faith looks like; there is an ease and strength behind decisions and actions. It is a strength gained from your journey into your vulnerability and emerging as a new being into the world. This strength connects you both to heaven and to earth. It grounds you in earth-power, bringing you depth and wisdom, and raises your vibration into spiritual awareness and enlightenment. You become the way of the new earth.

Connecting More Fully and Deeply with the Earth

The world is changing profoundly right now. We are witnessing changes in climate, environment, and human social structures and norms. Humans are evolving and it is a messy process right now.

Many people are changing at a fundamental and cellular level. I know that I have endured many years of being profoundly influenced by the solar, lunar, and planetary cycles, as well as other cosmic events I neither know nor understand.

STAGE 7: REINTEGRATION

Artist: Katia Honour

I have also been through an intense cleansing process within my auric field. A purging of old programming, entities and implants of age-old dark energetic forms are systematically being exposed and removed from my system. It is a disciplined process of paying attention and attending to what is happening within me at this moment. And nature and the earth, are my allies.

I know many people going through a similar process of connecting more fully and deeply with the earth. It is like the earth is growing up within them. It's not something they are trying to do; it is just something that is happening naturally. They are paying attention to their calling and allowing the process of growth and change to unfold.

Old ways of being, thinking and perceiving, are being shed, however reluctantly, allowing space for new growth to bud, slowly establish itself and then flourish.

A whole new certainty evolves. This new structure brings a whole new awareness and contentment into being as the new growth finally anchors more deeply and fully into the earth.

This is where many are becoming more connected to trees, to rocks, to sitting on the earth, and to listening to the sounds and rhythms of nature. As this 'ease of flow' becomes integrated within them, they bring this beingness into their ordinary day-to-day lives, enhancing all around them.

So, slow down, breathe, and feel your Self calling up from the earth, bringing strength, awareness and ease into the world. This is the change and the wisdom you want to see, and it emanates through you.

The Power of Surrender and Acceptance

The power of surrendering to life is not a passive one. It is an immensely courageous way of engaging the power of your vulnerability.

Surrendering to what life brings you, is an active motion of acknowledging and then accepting that there are powers greater than your desires and will.

Freedom and access to new power come from this state of surrender, but paradoxically, you must know *when* to allow it, and *when* not to. This is stepping into wisdom by applying your intuition and discernment.

Note well, this is not giving up; it is just giving up the resistance and willingness to fight what is happening.

To surrender spiritually means you give up your own will and allow your thoughts, ideas, and deeds to be guided by the will of a higher power.

Spiritual surrender is wilful acceptance and a yielding to a greater energy and force than you know. This begins the process of opening you to the power of service.

The highest emanations and maturity of the great archetypes; the Sovereign (Queen/King), the Warrior, and the Magician, are all there to serve. They serve high ideals and virtues and apply them in their daily lives. They serve the greater healing and welfare of all, and they do so, having fulfilled their own Hero's Journey; coming from innocence to wisdom through their ordeals, and then through humility, into service.

*"You know the trauma has dissolved,
when the very thought of the memory,
brings a warmth and smile to your heart ♥"*

An Exercise in Appreciation

There is a difference between romantic love and soul-based love.

Try this exercise: Imagine your lover, standing in front of you saying their words of love and adoration to you. Notice how that feels.

Then imagine them instead, standing beside you, looking into a mirror *with* you, seeing you, seeing your journey, and *then* saying their words of love and appreciation to you.

Big difference.

In the first scenario, you don't really *see* yourself. You see someone else in front of you saying their words of love and appreciation to you. It feels good without doubt, having someone you love, tell you they love you too, is a wonderful feeling and experience.

But in the second scenario, you *see* yourself. In *seeing* yourself, you experience the acceptance and appreciation of yourself, by you, *and* your beloved. This can be both a confronting and humbling experience. It can be a true breaking open into love.

For me, the process of self-acceptance and self-love has meant going on a journey through my suffering of illness, poverty, and powerlessness,

Artist: Ryoji Iwata

primarily on my own. But now I know and appreciate that this was part of my transformation process. I know it was about breaking old patterns and cycles from life-times past, feeling them, healing them and emerging from them. I thereby fulfilled huge soul contracts and agreements made before I was born.

I can now look in the mirror, and honestly say words of love, appreciation, and honour to my Self. I know I can say, "I see you. I appreciate you. I honour you. I honour your journey. I love you, and I thank you."

I now see the whole journey as about respecting and honouring the power of my Self, to endure my journey, and emerge from it as someone embodying my full Self.

I now understand how alchemy and the Hero's Journey are real processes of transformation and change. They work through human beings to clear energy and raise the vibration of the Earth. This process brings more golden energies of love, appreciation, and gratitude into the world. Something that truly creates the change in the world we so much want to see.

Relaxation: The Key to Breakthrough and Achievement

Relaxing is one of the most important keys to achievement and personal and spiritual breakthrough. Learning to relax in such a way that you allow the release of the tension in your mind and body, is both a skill and a discipline. When practised, it means you are truly present in more situations in your life, and therefore more able to bring your greatest wisdom and presence to the moment.

When you truly relax and can feel the flow of life and energy through your body, it creates a sense of newness and relief within you. You can feel the weight of your tension, and then your defences and armour can fall away. It reveals your willingness and ability to be your authentic self, in this moment.

This kind of relaxation doesn't come from watching TV or having a day-spa session, it is a dedicated practice that provides you with more ease, freedom and acceptance in your life. That is, if you can relax, even in difficult situations, your thoughts and behaviour stay open and available, rather than shutting down and closing off in survival mode.

It's one of the things I've learnt to do more and more in my teaching career, learn how to relax more in the classroom. This relaxed and calm energy I embody, then flows through to the students, who know they too are safe and can also relax. This makes learning easier and more fun for everyone.

It makes relationships easier too, as communication becomes about openness and sharing, rather than defending and reacting.

Most importantly, relaxation allows for the opening of a channel within yourself. This channel connects your spirit, heart and soul, and allows for an opening to healing and loving. And the world can always do with more of that.

It is Ok to Rest, Relax and Recuperate

Sometimes it really is okay, just to allow yourself to rest, relax and recuperate. This 'nothing' you are doing is the healthiest, strongest, and most loving action you can do. This is what preparation for a new, more vibrant and aware stage of life looks like.

This stage of releasing old concerns, causes, habits and toxins within your body is so important to creating the *new* being that is you. And it is all done by relaxing and enjoying doing 'nothing'.

It is especially important for those who were previously so active, achievement or goal-oriented, and those who determinedly put others' concerns ahead of their own. It is the same for those who want to *save the world* through some project or action, business or cause.

Sometimes though, it really is just time to rest, to allow the new to present itself in its own time and its own way. You really are moving into a more human, humble, and appreciative stage of awakening and awareness. And it is arriving according to its own timetable.

'Awakening' then is not about telling people about all the super levels of awareness, reciting texts or quotations, or eating the *rightest diet*. It is about the humble integration of energy that raises your vibration, while you are walking through your ordinary life. It means then that just your very presence is the healing agent for the people you connect with.

This is embracing the way of the new, the new fifth-dimensional state of being. And you are the embodiment of that state of being. And it is this that changes the world.

Out Beyond Ideas of Wrong-Doing and Right-Doing

Out beyond ideas of wrong-doing and right-doing,
there is a field. I'll meet you there.
When the soul lies down in that grass, the world is too
full to talk about. Ideas, language, even the phrase
'each other' doesn't make any sense.

–Rumi

STAGE 7: REINTEGRATION

I never really understood this oft shared and repeated quote from Rumi, until the election of Donald Trump as President of the United States. Now I know. I get it.

It's about moving out of a pattern of blame, rightness and righteousness, always getting what you want, and living in time-bound busyness and scarcity. This is the field of "ideas of wrong-doing and right-doing".

Trump exemplifies these old ways of polarity, achievement and entitlement, and for many, is a symbol of when 'America was Great'. Of course, this pattern requires great effort and energy to remain in place. It cannot exist long-term in an expansive world of diversity, change, inter-connectedness and continuing spiritual expansion and evolution.

The new way is about moving us into a place of experiencing and appreciating the field of All That Is. It is about moving us into a place of acceptance and non-judgement. It is about transcending the paradigm of 'fighting' and 'being right' and making the 'other' wrong. It is moving us beyond ideas of fairness and judgement and separation, and into the place of freedom, and ease of being where we are, right now. This is human evolution.

It is knowing that everything is alright, even if it is uncomfortable and not what you would prefer right now. This movement does not come from someone's intellect or desire, but brings forth a sense of well-being and profound harmony with All That Is.

It is the movement from the *fourth dimension* of thought, belief, emotion, and time, into the *fifth dimension*, which is beyond all of that. To do so, there must be emptying and then opening to a whole structure and way of being.

You must surrender all of your past ways of being and thinking and doing, to a path that is bigger than what you think or understand. This is the *work*, and this is the Journey. And it is painful. It is a process of natural growth and expansion. It is evolution.

During the 2016 US election campaign, I was amazed at the volume, intensity and the vehemence of the hatred directed towards Hillary Clinton. "She's a criminal!", "Killary is a murderer!", "The most corrupt politician ever!" Righteous people all of them, declaring their beliefs loudly and passionately.

These people are passionately engaged in the field of 'ideas of wrong-doing and right-doing'. And they will fight and fight and fight until their 'right' ideas and ideals are heard and acted upon. And the world will be a better place, right?

No. No, it won't. It keeps the world in a place of separation, lack and fear, of reaction and response. It keeps the world in the same old paradigm and structure that got us to where we are right now. As Einstein said, "You cannot solve your problems with the same thinking you used when you created them."

But letting go and moving on from your passionately held and long-researched beliefs is painful. It is the death of an identity. The death and destruction of your Known World. And the ego is programmed *not* to allow itself to die. It is programmed to defend territory and resist death on all levels. This is the reaction of the Warrior within you. This stage of letting go feels like 'giving up', like a great defeat that humiliates you. But giving up and surrendering are not the same.

"Giving up is refusing to participate in your experience. Surrender is ending your fight against your experiences, even if your experiences continue fighting you. In surrender, you are not giving up, but giving up your fight against the discomfort of outcome and circumstance." Matt Kahn, spiritual teacher.

So, if you want to change the world, love yourself, appreciate and value yourself first. *You* then become the change that will influence the world. Do this every day, and as often as you can.

It takes a *lot* of energy and intent to control outcomes and make the world and other people the way you want them to be. Bullies do this. But to release this desire and intent to control your environment, allows you to move into that field beyond thought and emotion, and into the freedom of allowing and knowing your true Self and your oneness with all.

This is the field where we are moving to. I will meet you there.

The Natural Nature of Emotions

Your emotions and the cycles of your development are normal and natural. Love and fear are both normal and natural emotions. So is anger and grief. They are part of the grief cycle. What causes you and others pain, is when you judge some emotions 'positive' and therefore 'good', and others 'negative' and therefore 'bad' and 'wrong'.

Your emotions and your stages of development are all natural. They are all colours within the spectrum of light. Some vibrations are visible and known, whilst others are not visible and are quite unconscious. What makes it hard though, is when you say some colours are good and acceptable, and others are not.

What makes it easier, is when you can consciously experience these emotions and stages of development, all the way through. When they are experienced all the way through, you complete a soul contract by transmuting that energy. This energy then moves out of your system, and into the greater space of Source energy.

Spiritual practices and mentors are only supposed to be there as guides, not rulers, controllers, or rule-makers. The spiritual ego though loves to create rules and practices where there is a definite system of 'right' and 'wrong', 'good' and 'bad', 'less than' and 'better than'. Eventually, you learn that you are not a servant to these teachers, practices and 'rules', they are there to serve you. These practices are there to serve you and your development, not the other way around.

The good thing is, we are all moving out of this stage and into a greater sense of freedom, expression, and abundance. This is the divine way that all those practices were leading us to in the first place.

A Taoist Parable

"Before enlightenment, chop wood and carry water. After enlightenment, chop wood and carry water."

A Taoist student had a question he passionately wanted answered. He searched and searched for a Master who could answer his question. He

*I love myself enough,
To feel my fear and uncertainty,
As a celebration,
Of my divine path unfolding.*

heard of a great monk, a revered master, who lived far away, who was said to be enlightened.

The student set off on his journey to meet the master and ask him his question. He travelled through many lands. He crossed flooded rivers, went through great rains, endured intense heat, cold and hunger. Finally, having walked over 800 miles, the student arrived at the village where the great Master lived.

The student found the Master in the fields, with his head down, tending his crops. Filled with joy, the student excitedly and humbly went up to the master and said, "Oh great master, I have walked over 800 miles across mountains and rivers and fields to ask you this question. Master, what is the key to a virtuous life?"

The Master just kept his head down and tended his crops.

This parable is teaching us about 'Waking Up'. It is teaching us that the immense effort we put into going on an arduous quest to find the answers to our questions, may be in service to an illusion. The illusion that our happiness and satisfaction will be attained only when we have achieved our goal, knowledge or quest. And waking up to this awareness, is humbling.

It is teaching us that enlightenment is about waking up from the illusions that held our attention and focus for so long. It is the awareness that the answer to the question, 'What is the key to a virtuous life?', is attending to your ordinary work, attending to the health and welfare of yourself and those around you, as best you can, here and now.

This is what Masters do. It is the application of their wisdom and enlightenment in their daily life. And it is done in service to the community.

'Enlightenment' isn't a revered, fixed state of being that sets you apart from others, but rather a process of humbling and unlearning, and then appreciating and applying in the world.

It really is true that, *"Before enlightenment, chop wood and carry water. After enlightenment, chop wood and carry water."*

Artist: Eduardo Prim

STAGE 7: REINTEGRATION

The Master and the Seeker

A Master
Sits comfortably in not-knowing.
The Seeker
Cannot sit comfortably,
Until they know everything.
The Master blesses.
The student seeks and strives
To become a Master.
The Master blesses.
The student finds the one path.
The Master blesses.
The student judges
Those who are not.
The Master blesses.
The student resists and resents.
The Master blesses.
The student fails,
Falls and dies.
The Master blesses.
A Master arises
And gives thanks.
The blessing is received.
The son rises.
It is a new day.

Changing Your State of Being - The Benefits of Meditation

As I moved through my journey and released more of my old patterns of thought and behaviour, I knew I had to apply my new awareness in my daily work. This meant applying different communication and teaching strategies in the classroom.

I began introducing meditation as a normal part of the class routine. At first, the students were uncertain of this new practice. The older ones, the grade 6 students especially, were self-conscious and hesitant, but the younger ones always responded best.

One day I was teaching Grade 2 (seven and eight-year-olds) and went about the normal classroom routine. We did some energetic singing and dancing to start the class, and then the students sat on the floor as I called the roll.

Now some kids find it hard to sit still, particularly boys, after some energetic activity. Their bodies just want to move around continually. It's not their fault, their bodies just want to move. On this day, one boy was literally rolling around on the floor.

After calling the roll, I normally take the kids through a short meditation, concentrating on awareness of breath, and the visualisation of a golden ball coming down through their bodies, absorbing and taking away stress and anxiety. It takes about two to three minutes.

Well, after this short time, this one little boy, who was previously rolling around on the floor, was now sitting tall and still, quiet and content. His state had literally changed in three minutes. His body was now calm and relaxed, and he was listening and aware.

It is amazing what a mindful activity can do in such a short period of time. This example shows me that simply doing meditation or any other spiritual activity doesn't change your circumstances, but it does allow you to experience your circumstances differently.

I can now experience the same circumstances in a calmer and more content way, rather than with stress, anxiety and a desire to control. I am in a place of allowing and acceptance, rather than tension and control. I achieve far more with greater ease than I ever did before. And those around me, especially the children, are also far more at ease and capable than they were before. I have become the change we want to see in the world.

Romantic Relationships - They Are Evolving

Relationships are changing, just like the environment. However, most people don't change with the environment, we want the environment to change for us.

As you grow and mature, and complete your soul contracts and soul's journey, you evolve into a more independent being. You are more generous, more open, more courageous, more self-directed, more curious and more humble. You don't *need* stuff anymore. You don't *need* the outside world, or even a romantic partner, to approve or affirm you anymore. You have been on your journey, gone through the times of hardship and turmoil, and emerged anew; stronger, more complex and more at ease with yourself and the world.

But all of this involves your journey and your work. It is your life's work to take responsibility for what is in your field; clear it, transmute it, and then move on to the next higher level of your purpose. The environment around you, is often what is needed to ensure you engage with your soul's work.

This may mean being born into a dysfunctional family, working in a high-pressure job, joining certain social groups, or establishing friendships or romantic partnerships with particular people through different stages in your life. But what happens when you complete these contracts and have done the healing and the clearing? What happens then?

Relationships are evolving. It's not about finding the *one* right person to be with for the rest of your life anymore. This may have served for a period, but it is changing as you are changing. Everything is deepening and becoming more complex, allowing for greater connection at higher and deeper levels of being.

The new way may involve extended periods of being alone. It may involve being deeply connected with someone, but not necessarily being physically near them. It is always about expanding your self-respect, your self-love, and your self-care, because this is how your wisdom and love are demonstrated in the world.

For me, I too love romance. But more so, I love the opportunity for silliness, intimacy, sensual expression, honesty and sharing. It provides the opportunity for me to be more fully my true self. This for me is a wonderfully rich, creative and loving expression.

New relationships are now more about providing a sacred vessel for you to each grow into and express your new-found complexity. It's not about how quickly you can get into bed and cohabitate with someone anymore. That was about neediness and the expression of woundedness.

You cannot lose by loving. You can and will be hurt for sure. And despite all of your efforts, this will happen, and relationships may not last. But that doesn't mean you have lost. It means you have experienced the depth and breadth of love; all of what it means to be in an expansive relationship.

Relationships are some of the hardest and most fulfilling experiences you will have in your lifetime. They are there to fill you up, tear you down and rip you apart. You will go through periods of absolute certainty and knowing, and then, periods of seemingly knowing nothing at all. You ask yourself, "Who am I? Who are you? What have I been doing for all these years? What happens next?"

And all of this is what is meant to happen. Relationships are there to help you become free. Free to be your true Self, your true expressive and most loving self. And sometimes, it's just bloody hard.

But after the healing, there is the opening. And in the opening, there lies the freedom. And in the freedom, there lies the power and the abundance, the satisfaction and contentment. Finally. And yes, I want some of that too.

"I'm so glad we kept walking this path together."

**George Harrison to Olivia
Harrison as he is dying of cancer.**

Maturity - Embodying the Purpose of our Lives

I've come to appreciate that maturity is really how we embody the purpose of our lives.

Maturity is the embodying of our wisdom and experience. We are now capable of enacting the virtues and principles we decided to learn as a soul before we were born.

And maturity only comes via experience, and this experience is gained through both our triumphs and our ordeals. It comes from falling in love, from the heartbreak of betrayal, to the joy of helping someone, to the elation of getting 'it', and to finally releasing fears and anxieties, facing our wounds and our Shadow, and moving into acceptance, meaning and peace.

Maturity comes from looking back and seeing your path and valuing your journey. It comes from acknowledging and finally welcoming *all* the disparate parts of your Self. It is welcoming and embracing all of those fragmented parts that have endured lifetimes of trauma and woundedness. They are welcomed back with heart-full thanks, acceptance and grace.

This is walking your path as the Courageous Vulnerable, and completing your Hero's Journey. It is realising that your 'work' in this lifetime is not about your job, your achievements, or how 'right' you lived, but about completing your soul-contracts. That's where the freedom lies, in accepting your soul-contracts and completing them.

This part of the Journey is like that scene in the forest in the last Harry Potter movie (The Deathly Hallows - Part 2) where Harry opens the 'Golden Snitch' as his final task in crossing the threshold to fulfil his purpose.

Harry gains the memories of Professor Snape, from the tears he shed when he was dying so painfully. The images from these memories showed Harry, however tortuously, that there had always been a much bigger picture at play, serving and protecting him throughout his life. Harry was shown, that many people made great sacrifices for him and the welfare of others, to bring about a greater vision of freedom for the world. This awareness was more than he could have known at the time. After all, he was just a kid, how could he know?

Through the gift of Snape's memories, Harry sees his path, the path that he *must* follow. It is revealed to him through these visions the sacrifice that *he* must make to fulfil his journey and ensure the success of the grand plan.

He sees his path and understands what he needs to do. He must die. He acknowledges his path, he knows it, and finally accepts it. He will walk his path. And in the forest scene, standing alone, he says, "I am ready to die". Only after speaking out this truth of his awareness of his path of sacrifice, does the Snitch "open at the close".

When it opens, it provides him with his final gift. The final gift he needs to fulfil his purpose. He sees his most loving guides who have been present with him throughout his life and ordeals. He knows they have been with him, loving him, always. He knows now, he is not alone, and never has been.

Maturity is then the acceptance of your journey, walking your path, and knowing there is a grand picture at play for you to bring forth your gifts into the world. It is knowing that, even through your hardest times, you were serving a grand purpose.

Suffering and Compassion

Channelling compassion is our greatest strength. Applying it is a major factor in bringing connection into the world. It is not the only connection between people, but also in the community. Bringing compassion in relationships is how you demonstrate your values of respect and love, and how you challenge yourself to grow and live out your truths.

It is the lack of compassion that causes shame and guilt to be projected onto others. It dwells within you. It maintains feelings of unsafety and insecurity and prolongs the energy of trauma in your body.

Demonstrating compassion, however, brings safety and allows people to release their shields and armour that have kept them feeling safe in vigilance and survival mode for so long.

The gateway to compassion is not through the Warrior codes of attacking and defending, armouring and perseverance, but in your vulnerability. It is through the Lover and the Caregiver archetypes that engage virtues like empathy, care, harmony and reverence. These are the powerful forces of the divine feminine in your life.

Artist: Katia Honour

Compassion appears when qualities that may have served you so well previously, like resistance and armouring, break down. This process provides the opening for your greatest qualities and essence to emerge. This is the archetypal process of birthing yourself anew. It brings forth character traits like trust, confidence and self-belief, which then can be transferred to others in your life and brought forth in your family and work life.

The capacity then to experience suffering, move into vulnerability, and then emerge as a more humble and greater being, strengthens your ability to continue your Hero's Journey and fulfil your soul's mission. Thus, can you gain the rewards and Cross the Threshold again, to go back into your former world with humility, wisdom, and maturity.

It is in your acknowledgement of your suffering that you create profound connection and support for others. When you are no longer afraid of experiencing your pain, and perhaps even your death, you open yourself to the gifts and power of your vulnerability. It is here that you open yourself to compassion, healing, and forgiveness. These are profound shifts and move you further on your journey into integrating these gifts into the world.

This is bringing forth your soul's purpose and the miracles that only you can bring into the world. This is the true meaning of living in light and love.

After the Healing - Freedom and Maturity

As you complete your journey and move into the final stage of The Return, you experience more times of serenity, empowerment and fun. You have endured the arduous times of struggle and uncertainty, and have emerged from your initiations through the darkness, whole, and complete.

And the traumas you experienced... after not too long... you start forgetting. You start forgetting those days of hardship and struggle. It becomes like a fog in your mind. "There's something there... but... I don't know... I can't quite remember it... I can't quite see it anymore. I am more interested in what is happening *now*", you say to yourself.

The sense and the memories of those times just leave. They just slip into the ocean of your life like the dissolution of a once-enormous iceberg.

And now, as the ocean of your field becomes clear again, you are at once, free to be part of more things and all things, and no things all at once. It is the ultimate expression of oneness.

But the great thing is, you retain the energy and wisdom of maturity; the growth, the compassion, the empathy, the depth of expression and

"This path to God has made me such an old sweet beggar. I was starving until one night my love tricked God to fall into my bowl. Now I'm infinitely rich but all I ever want to do is keep emptying out my emerald-filled pockets upon this tear-stained world."

~ **Hafiz**

appreciation, all without the emotional triggering and need for defences. You are just a more all-encompassing being than ever before. You are content just to be you.

The journey reveals your name, your true name and essence, as well as the gifts you bring into the world.

This is where wisdom comes from: from experiencing your journey through the shadow and the dark, and then back up into the light, bringing the awareness and growth back to earth and into the community. It is the tale of the Wounded Healer, who becomes a Master, by healing themselves, and then bringing this healing into the world. It is a powerful and courageous tale.

A Simple Connection

I remember when I met Colin. He was standing outside a property hitchhiking into town on the Sunshine Coast hinterland. He engaged me straight away as he got into my car. He was a guy in his late sixties, all dried-up, cracked skin and joyful expression. A sprightly fellow who had probably emptied a few too many Jim Beams in his life.

"Thanks for stoppin' mate. You can drop me anywhere in town", he said.

He was wearing an old thin t-shirt and shorts of good quality material. He sat easily in the car, very much at home. He talked about cars, the old ones from the 50s with the wings, and his work. He spoke rapidly and with good humour.

"Ya know, I work in house painting, and I don't want a big car. Something like this or a Mazda would suit me fine. I mean why people buy those big 4-wheel drive beasts I don't know. Maybe if you're on a property an' got a steep driveway. I only need to have something to fit a seven-foot ladder in. I mean, yeah, you'd get one in here no worries. Everything else you can just hire and deliver on site."

Colin was easy to chat to. He spoke with a confident flow, rattling off ideas and thoughts.

I dropped him off at the bus stop in town. He was genuinely pleased with our conversation and I think he would have liked to continue.

"Good conversation. Thanks, mate. Ya know", he paused, "I wouldn't have had this opportunity if I had me own car. I think I'll keep hitchin' for a while. See ya." He got out of the car and waved goodbye.

I drove off to do my shopping and thought appreciatively of this short connection with a fellow I wouldn't normally have had a chance to speak to. He showed me how we all live in different worlds and have our own journeys to follow. He showed me a man with a sincere desire for connection, and he was open and willing to do so. He wasn't guarded or cynical but was genuinely curious and interested in sharing his thoughts and engaging with someone.

Or he may have been lonely and was just finding a simple way to connect with someone. Either way, connection is the heart of community. If we aren't willing to make connections, and have the courage to do so, we will live isolated, lonely and disconnected lives, even though we may have big cars, steep driveways and grand jobs. Thank you, Colin. I hope your car stays at the mechanics for a little while longer.

STAGE 7: REINTEGRATION

Questions and Exercises:

1. Give some thought as to when, where and how you experienced a 'Reintegration' in your life.
   - Name two occasions when you know you experienced a Reintegration.
   - What were the gifts and the pressures the Reintegration brought to you?
   - What 'triggered' the Reintegration?
   - What archetypes did the Reintegration bring up for you? Eg: the Hero, the Saboteur, the Healer, the Magical Child, the Prostitute, the Rescuer, the Teacher, the Warrior etc?
2. Looking back, what three things do you think you were supposed to learn from your Reintegration?
3. How did you respond to the various trials and challenges you were presented during your Reintegration? Name two that you know you responded well to, and two that you know you didn't respond well.
4. What pressures were upon you to make decisions during your Reintegration?
   - How did you make your decisions?
   - Did you respond with grandiosity or with humility and clarity?
5. Name three things from this part of the book that moved you or struck you as important.
6. Creative expression - drawing: Take some time to find a quiet space. Breathe deeply and relax your body. Feel the breath go all the way through your body, and clear your mind. With paper, coloured pencils or crayons in front of you, ask yourself clearly, "Show me what is important for me to know from this part of the book."

Then, with your non-dominant hand, choose a pencil or crayon, and start drawing. It doesn't matter what it looks like, just create. Change hands when your body tells you. Repeat.

Conclusion - "Whom does the Hero's Journey serve?"

We live in a world of ordinary heroes. They are your mother, your husband, your wife, the guy next door, the young woman across the street, even those pesky teenage kids; they are everywhere. They are here and now, they were with you last week, and they will be with you next month. And there is also a hero looking back at you in the mirror, as uncomfortable as that may sound to some.

We all go through a journey in our lives, mostly unconsciously, to achieve our life's mission and purpose. The Hero's Journey is a universal template describing the stages we go through on this journey.

It describes a purpose and cycle which is bigger than what we consciously know or understand at the time. It shows us a natural cycle that takes us into achievement and transformation by way of challenges, hardship, and the courage to go to our depths.

To go through this journey, and to ultimately achieve your grand purpose in life, there is a price to pay. There is always a price to pay. And this price will open you to the courage needed to listen to and heed the *call*, the Call to Adventure and go on your Journey.

This book describes some of the many pathways, pitfalls, and ways to wisdom of an ordinary, courageous hero (You) as they go on their life's journey.

With the oncoming of the coronavirus in early 2020, I believe we are in a time of worldwide Initiation. This is a time of great change and the

CONCLUSION - "WHOM DOES THE HERO'S JOURNEY SERVE?"

crossing of a threshold into the Unknown World. This has happened without our conscious consent and has brought great loss and grief, as people around the world deal with the loss of loved ones, jobs, routines, businesses, households, certainty, and connection with others.

This time will herald a period of unprecedented change throughout the world.

It is why the Hero's Journey and other universal templates of transformation like alchemy, are even more relevant today.

By engaging with the Hero's Journey consciously, you can more easily and comprehensively move through it. Certain stages will always be painful, but they become more manageable as you are aware that you are engaging a profound and natural cycle in your life. It is the level of consciousness you bring to this process that determines whether you suffer through your sufferings, or move through them with a level of ease and acceptance..

It is important to note that, often you will not know what the issues you need to work through on your journey are, until you have moved through them. Mostly they are issues arising in your childhood. Sometimes these issues are well defined, other times they are an amorphous sense or feeling within your body or field. You know something is there, but you don't know what it is.

In the Grail myth of The Fisher King, Parsifal, the young and innocent Knight, after enduring his journey through battles with dragons and saving damsels and townsfolk for many years, he must ask the question that will set him, The Fisher King and the realm free: "Whom does the Grail serve?"

What does that mean? What is the purpose of the Holy Grail and whom does it serve?

The answer comes back as, "The Grail serves the Grail King."

What does this mean and who is the Grail King?

The Grail serves the highest and most sovereign being in the land, to help them fulfil their purpose and their aims. This purpose is to care for the realm, ensure it is prosperous, that boundaries are maintained and there is a balance between power and freedom, heaven and earth.

For you, the "Grail King" means *your* highest and most divine self. It is your most Sovereign self. The Grail King is the one who lives within you (whatever your gender), the one who is hidden behind all the wounds, armour and bravado.

Naturally, this question also applies to the Hero's Journey. "Whom does the Hero's Journey serve?"

The answer is that it serves your highest and most sovereign self that resides within you. The Hero's Journey serves your highest and most noble self to achieve your life's purpose and bring you fulfilment, love, prosperity and freedom.

It is humbling to know that we only learn of our great inner being of power and nobility, after we have endured our journey, been humbled, and fulfilled our duty.

It is also important to note that in The Fisher King, Parsifal has only to ask the question to receive the rewards, he does not have to know the answer. It is in the sincere and humble asking then, that provides the rewards and the fulfilment of your purpose. It is this sincere intention to serve a higher purpose, made in the awareness of your current reality, that you receive the gifts of your greatness.

The Hero's Journey is still relevant today. It is especially so in these times of great change. It is a timeless expression of our human need to live a life of purpose and fulfilment. And it is true for women and men of any age and culture.

It shows us that the purpose of life is not happiness or the achievement of our grandiose goals and missions, but to serve this centre of divine power and grace within us, and bring that service into the world. From here will our happiness and abundance flow.

And thence, a new journey begins.

Acknowledgements

This book draws upon material from many years of work. To bring it to fruition, I am very grateful for the work of my first editor Travis Earsman. He provided the initial sounding board for me to organise my ideas and material, and provide the impetus and motivation to collate, arrange and cull an unruly bunch of articles into a coherent structure. Thank you.

I would also like to acknowledge Emily Gowor and her team who enabled me to continue the process of bringing this book into creation.

I also wish to express my appreciation to the many people who have supported my writing over the years. It was that initial feedback that let me know that my thoughts and expressions were appreciated and would make a valuable contribution to the world.

And finally, I would like to express my great appreciation for the artists who have granted me permission to use their work.

Leo Plaw, His work is Arise. See more of Leo's work at www.LeoPlaw.com

Katia Honour. See more of Katia's work at www.katiahonour.com

Steve de la Mare. See more of Steve's work at www.artstation.com/stevedelamare.

About the Author:

Matthew Harris is a long-time teacher, storyteller, workshop presenter and writer who lives and works in the beautiful Byron Bay region of New South Wales.

He writes inspirational articles and gives workshops on the Hero's Journey, spirituality and personal transformation. He helps people find inspiration, purpose and meaning in their lives by helping them appreciate themselves and their heroic and noble journeys in life.

Matthew has experienced his own Hero's Journey, encountering extended periods of illness, depression and poverty. This was an Initiation experience that introduced him powerfully to his limitations, but eventually, lead him into breakthroughs that brought about his emergence, through humility, into his gifts, talents and wisdom.

He has been interested in mythology, spirituality, and the archetypal path since childhood. Through his studies and work experience, he combines these elements to provide a roadmap for human growth, transformation and fulfilment.

Matthew provides seminars, retreats, workshops and courses in writing, spiritual teaching, and the Way of the Courageous Vulnerable – How to Find Meaning and Purpose From the 7 Stages of the Hero's Journey in your daily life. His courses and programs provide participants access to their inherent wisdom and power, and fulfils their basic need to find self-value, self-appreciation and purpose.

Matthew believes that we all go through a journey in our lives, mostly unconsciously, to achieve our life's mission and purpose. Matthew's work reveals this inner courage and nobility within your own heart.

This is his first book.

www.ingramcontent.com/pod-product-compliance
Lightning Source LLC
Chambersburg PA
CBHW040740020526
44107CB00083B/2811